The Sporting Mirror

1881-86

A History, Index and Bibliography

Chris Harte

This Book has been Published in a Limited Edition
of Fifty copies of which this is Number 46

Sports History Publishing

Harry Etherington

Etherington's Fleet Street office
was on the third floor

Sports History Publishing

First published in 2020

ISBN : 978-1-898010-12-8

Editor : Susan Lewis

Consultant Editor : Kiri Wood

Cover : Rupert Cavendish

Layout : Proprint of Carmarthen

Contact : chrismedia47@yahoo.co.uk

Printed and bound in Wales

Recent Books by the Author include

The Sporting Mirror: A History, Index and Bibliography (2020)
Hunting in Carmarthenshire 1741-1975 (2019)
An Index and Bibliography of Baily's Magazine (2017)
A Season With the Carmarthenshire Hunt (2016)
Old Gold: Carmarthen Town Football Club (2013)
Watching Brief (2010)
Recollections of a Sportswriter (2009)
The History of Australian Cricket (2008)
Rugby Clubs and Grounds (2005)
English Rugby Clubs (2004)
Britain's Rugby Grounds (2003)
Australian Cricket History (2003)
Reminiscences of a Sportswriter (2002)
Menston Actually (2001)
Sports Books in Britain (2000)
Ramblings of a Sportswriter (1999)
A Year in the Sporting Pressbox (1998)
The Twickenham Papers (1997)
A Sportswriter's Year (1997)
Sporting Heritage (1996)
One Day in Leicester (1995)
A History of Australian Cricket (1993)
Cricket Indulgence (1991)
History of South Australian Cricket (1990)
South African International Cricket (1989)
Two Tours and Pollock (1988)
Seven Tests (1987)
Australians in South Africa (1987)
Cricket Safari (1986)
Australian Cricket Journal (1985)
Cricket Rebels (1985)
The History of the Sheffield Shield (1984)
The Fight for the Ashes (1983)
Cathedral End (1979)

In Preparation

A History, Index and Bibliography of The Captain Magazine
(to be published in 2021)

INTRODUCTION AND ACKNOWLEDGEMENTS

The Sporting Mirror was first published in late January 1881. The title page noted it as being 'Volume 1, January to June,' yet the first page has it as being the February number. This confusion continued until the final, sixtieth, issue which was dated January 1886. The initial publisher was Harry Etherington with the editor being Henry Bromhead and the office was on the third floor of 152 Fleet Street which is situated in the heart of what used to be London's newspaper world.

In July 1885, with circulation falling, Etherington decided to concentrate on his various cycling publications and he sold *The Sporting Mirror* to Palmer & Son of Paternoster Row. Although Bromhead continued as editor until the end of the year the new owners decided to make various alterations. The typeface was changed although the basic layout remained the same. The portraits and sometimes obsequious biographies were pared to a minimum with sporting sketches introduced. New contributors were added to the list of regular writers but after a further six issues it became obvious that the publication had failed to generate any extra interest into what was an already crowded sporting magazine market. After sixty issues *The Sporting Mirror* folded without giving any warning to its readers.

It should be noted that where Biographies are noted as being written by 'HBB' this, obviously, is the editor Henry Brown Bromhead. However, many other articles, for which there are no credited writers, can generally be assumed to be Bromhead's work. His output was prodigious even allowing for the fact he was supplying a large amount of copy at the time to the Sunday sporting newspaper *The Referee.*

Harry Generes Banks (1862-1947) was an artist and lithographer who spent his whole working life in studios based around Soho in central London. He drew all of the portraits and lithographs which appeared in *The Sporting Mirror.*

*   *   *   *   *

Henry John Etherington, always known as Harry, was born on 1st September 1855 in Sittingbourne, Kent. His father, Henry Walker Etherington, was the captain of a number of boats which plied their trade on the Rivers Medway and Thames. His mother Jane, nee Powell, was the daughter of a Faversham farmer who, as was the custom of the time to raise large families, gave birth to seven children.

Harry, as the eldest boy, was sent to boarding school in Canterbury where he

became fascinated with the written word and was soon appointed as editor of the school magazine. He left school in 1871 and spent a short time working on boats with his father. Being unable to devote much time to writing he left home and travelled to London to try and find employment in newspapers. Fortunately, one of his mother's sisters lived with her husband in a big manse in St.Pancras where Harry was given a room until he found his feet.

He was soon employed as a journalist where his enthusiasm gained him a number of influential friends. He began to ride the velocipede (an early form of bicycle propelled by pushing along the ground with the feet) in the mid-1860s and then, subsequently, the bicycle. In later times a contemporary said of him: "To give even a brief outline of Mr Etherington's career would be to write the history of the sport of cycling."

Harry became deeply involved in the sport initially as a journalist and publisher followed by that of a promoter. Above all he was an entrepreneur, selling the fast growing sport of cycling to the general public. He started his first cycling newspaper in 1876 when, with a small loan from his aunt, he took an office in Whitefriars Street in the City of London. The initial title was *Bicycling News* which, a year later, became *Bicycling Times*. It was printed by Adlards of Bartholomew Close, West Smithfield in the City and priced at 2d.

From its inception it was intended to be 'a high-class periodical with illustrations, sketches and engravings devoted to this popular pastime.' Initially Etherington was editor as well as the owner but in 1882 he appointed Charles James Fox as editor. In January 1884, Fox changed the name to *Cycling Times* and with various minor title changes it continued until 1897.

However, unknown to Etherington, an employee, Alfred Harmsworth (later Lord Northcliffe), was misusing the newspaper's paper and presses for his own ends. Appointed editor in 1886, at the age of twenty-one, Harmsworth came to dislike working for Etherington and was soon planning to launch his own titles. Behind the back of his employer he started *Answers*, his first magazine. By stealing newsprint he managed to increase the circulation without cost until Etherington found out what was going on and fired Harmsworth.

In 1878 Harry published *'Etherington and Co's Bicyclists Directory, Exchange and Guide'* in which he described himself as an 'Advertising Agent.' The following year he published *The Sporting Annual* (subtitled 'A complete and comprehensive record of every sporting and athletic feat.') as well as *The Bicycle Annual for 1879*. Etherington's business activities were clearly growing at a rapid pace and he had to move offices in order to accommodate his growing staffing levels.

His other titles included *Cyclist*, with Henry Sturmey and Charles Nairn as editors using Iliffe, a Coventry based firm, as printers. Both editors also took charge of *The Wheel World* when Etherington and Lacy Hillier started it in May

1880. Other titles included *London Wheeling, The Lady Cyclist, The Cycle* and, in 1884, *Wheeling*. There were many other short lived publications and Annuals right up to the start of the war of 1914.

Etherington made his name in late 1879 when he promoted long distance cycling races in America. He offered large sums of money for the winners but with the craze growing rapidly, and tens of thousands of spectators paying to watch his races, he returned to London a wealthy man. His tour of 1885 was an even greater financial success.

In between all of this he found time to marry twenty year old Alice Grieves in May 1882 at St.Saviour's Church in South Hampstead. He had purchased a house at 135 Camden Street, St.Pancras two years earlier but after Alice produced four boys (Cyril, Ernest, Henry and Ralph) the family moved to a larger property at 10 Steele's Road, South Hampstead which was situated a short distance from his in-law's home.

Alice did not enjoy good health after the birth of Ralph, her fourth child, and somewhat reluctantly Harry purchased, in 1895, a sea-front property on Grand Parade, Eastbourne in order for his wife to live with the sea air. He found commuting to his Fleet Street office took up too much of his working day and subsequently purchased a London residence in Willesden Lane, Brondesbury Park. Alice continued to live in Eastbourne until her death in 1930, which was not long after Harry had sold his London home and purchased a typical Sussex cottage in Bedfordwell Road. He died at the house in August 1938, only days after having been fined ten shillings at Eastbourne Magistrates Court for driving a car without having a licence.

Although Etherington is remembered as 'the father of British cycling,' especially for his various publications and secretaryship of London's Temple Bicycling Club, he also started a number of other publications of which *The Sporting Mirror* is the subject of this book.

Henry Brown Bromhead was born in a tied cottage in St.Mary's Street, Stamford, Lincolnshire in August 1852. He attended Stamford School where his literary ability shone through. As a youth he travelled widely with his father, Richard, who worked at nearby Burghley House training horses for the Cecil family. On his father's death in 1871, Henry gave up his minor post as a Junior Master at his school and moved to London where he obtained employment on *The Sporting Life* newspaper under the editorship of Harry Feist.

At the time of Feist's death in 1874, and that of his star writer Henry Hall Dixon, the standard of sports journalism had risen to new heights. The paper had also seen the departure of Edward Dorling who, for twelve years, had been Feist's right-hand man as well as Martin Cobbett known for his rustic column 'Man on the March.' Bromhead had learnt a lot from these fine men and when offered a

position on *The Referee*, by his old school colleague Henry Sampson, he decided to make the move. He soon became known as 'Boris,' the name above his regular Turf articles which continued until his death twenty years later.

Baily's Magazine of Sports and Pastimes, when writing about Bromhead stated: "He was a man of fine physique," which might well explain his rather complicated private life. On his move to London he resided in Wynne Road, Brixton and within a short time married a woman named Lilian at Brixton Parish Church. It seems that they stayed together for about sixteen years before Lilian disappeared from his life. Extensive research has found no notification of death or divorce. However, a woman of the same name and age appears on the Australian Government's immigration lists for 1888 in the company of a George Brown.

Whatever the marital situation Bromhead had risen in stature and was able, in 1878, to purchase a property in George Street (now north Gower Street) in St.Pancras. He stayed there until his separation from Lilian after which he brought a splendid Georgian house in Guilford Street, Bloomsbury. A contemporary comment stated: "The street housed many artists, authors and engineers along with lawyers and architects."

In August 1891 he married for a second time and moved to St.George's Mansions in Red Lion Square. His bride was twenty year old Jessie Stevens and the ceremony took place at St.Peter's Church in Regent's Square. Jessie had been born in Poole, Dorset where her father, George, was involved in boat building. She moved to London, firstly going into domestic service and latterly being employed in the office of *The Referee* in a clerical position.

The marriage lasted for less than three years as Henry died in his Holborn office on 6 March 1894 at the relatively young age of forty-one. His interment took place four days later at St.Marylebone Cemetery in East Finchley. Jessie did not hang around for too long, selling the home and moving in with Walter Jones in Barking Road, Plaistow, some time before their wedding. In 1907 the couple left the east end of London and purchased a sea-front property in Kings Road, Brighton.

The obituaries of Bromhead showed how respected he had become. *Baily's Magazine*, in its April 1894 issue stated: "He appeared to have many years of life before him, yet he succumbed after an illness of a few days. Henry Bromhead was a keen sportsman at heart and had made a study of sporting history especially in connection with Turf matters. Over the signature of 'Boris' he, for a long series of years, wrote the Turf articles in *The Referee*. Other articles of his, especially in *The Sporting Mirror*, were signed 'Diomed' while to the pages of the *Licensed Victuallers' Gazette* he contributed a great number of racing articles and histories of famous racehorses. For our own pages here in *Baily's Magazine* he had frequently written a variety of interesting papers."

The Referee, in their edition of 11 March 1894, ran a lengthy article on the funeral and mourners stating: "The hearse and carriages, which started from the home of the deceased, were met at the cemetery by a very large gathering of friends and colleagues, representatives of sport and of the sporting press. The funeral service was conducted by the vicar of St.Peter's Church, Grays Inn Road. The coffin of polished oak bore the inscription 'Henry Brown Bromhead. Died 6 March 1894.'"

"Among those present at the graveside were the deceased's brother John Bromhead and his sister Elizabeth along with over three dozen sporting journalists and many friends. Wreaths and crosses of beautiful flowers, which had completely covered the coffin, were placed round the open grave. Among those who sent such tokens of affection, respect and regret was the widow 'to my darling husband from his sorrowing wife.' Others were from various family members, the staff of *The Referee*, the compositors of *The Referee* and the proprietors of the *Licensed Victuallers' Gazette*."

The article named over fifty others who were present including Martin Cobbett, Edward Spencer Mott, Phil May, Frank Butler, Henry Custance, Edward Cuming, Arthur Binstead, John Corlett, Finch Mason, Alfred Watson and William Blew. It concluded saying: "Prior to the ceremony the weather, which had been gloomy, brightened up, and when, amidst sunshine and flowers, the coffin was lowered, a bright gleam enabled the sorrowing crowd to take a long lingering look on the casket which contained all that was mortal of the man they loved so well."

$$* \quad * \quad * \quad * \quad *$$

The first issue of *The Sporting Mirror* contained an introduction on the first two pages. It read as follows:

"So great is the desire for the higher class of literature in this age of progress, that new works and editions are daily bursting on the scene. Some come like a thunderclap on our sportive little world, perhaps to die away as rapidly as they arrive. Others with steady progress and quiet demeanour make their mark and gain a sound foundation before we are even aware of their existence."

"Glancing round we find books and papers in every hole and corner; on every table and bookstall, both in our houses and in the streets. The majority of these supply wants that would otherwise be plainly deficient to the narrowest observer. In presenting *THE SPORTING MIRROR* to our readers we do so with a quiet resolution and sound intention, to fill up the niche awaiting an occupant, that is at the present time existing in the sporting literature of our country."

"The world of sport has increased very rapidly of late years. The names of the celebrities of the racecourse, the river, the running path and the cricket field are as household words in the majority of English homes. Years ago a man who indulged

in athletic pursuits was, to a certain extent, considered a pariah or an outcast from the ranks of society."

"Now it is quite the other way. Athletic ability is, in many instances, thought a recommendation rather than otherwise. Our sisters and our cousins now join with us more and more in our various pastimes as successive seasons glide away, consequently the names of our leading performers possess a world-wide reputation, and are freely mentioned in the course of our everyday conversations."

"A quarter of a century ago ten or twelve persons indulged in sporting practices, where hundreds and thousands follow the popular craze at the present day. What may be termed the march of civilisation by the introduction of athletic pursuits into our educational establishments, causes the number of votaries to be steadily increasing. Both in our business intercourse and in the seclusion of our homes we are being continually reminded of the world of sport by many passing events and this proves its sustained prosperity and wide-known popularity."

"The modern day literature sharpens our appetites by recording the doings of all the sporting world and eagerly, like flies to the web, we plunge deeper and deeper into its attractions. If we are not able to be present, with what pleasure do we read accounts and descriptions of a well contested horse or foot race, or the finish of a close and exciting cricket match."

"How we always regret not having witnessed it whilst we imagine that we know the forms and figures of the principals as if they were amongst the ranks of our nearest and dearest friends."

"Still, after all, there seems something wanting that we do not seem to satisfy. We possess some inward craving to know more about these champions and celebrities whom we are constantly reading about yet very seldom see. We are anxious to preserve some memento to act as a recollection of their doings. At the present time there is nothing in the whole library of English literature that will enable us to satisfy this desire."

"It is to supply this void, to fill up this niche, that has caused us to place *THE SPORTING MIRROR* into the hands of the public. Within its pages they will find lifelike portraits of the men they consider heroes in the world of sport. Biographies are also published containing accounts of their performances and narrating many incidents of their career, both in the arena and in their private life."

"Besides these, articles written by competent authorities and the recognised critics of every sporting pursuit will also be printed on its leaves. No stone will be left unturned to make *THE SPORTING MIRROR* the best and most complete work amongst the whole of the literature on the pastimes of the time. As a record alone it will stand unsurpassed."

"A correct and complete return of the doings of the month will be kept in tabular form, easy of reference and containing all the information the inquirer desires.

Future events will be treated in like manner so that all information concerning the doings of the time to come can be obtained at once."

"The success of *THE SPORTING MIRROR* rests entirely with ourselves. In presenting the first number to our readers we do so with confidence, thinking that little fault will be found with the work. Still, we shall not rest on our labours. Fresh events are constantly occurring; fresh ideas are continually forming and these we shall take advantage of so as to add further to the benefit and welfare of our subscribers."

"If any of our readers should take the slightest exception to our principles; if any can offer suggestions as to the improvement of our book, we shall only be too happy to take into consideration all propositions from whatever source they may emanate. If we think them worthy of acknowledgment, and that *THE SPORTING MIRROR* would be improved thereby, we shall at once act accordingly and the proposer of such alteration will always possess our warmest approbation and most sincere thanks."

A year later, under the heading 'To Our Readers,' Bromhead wrote: "Twelve months have passed away since the first issue of *THE SPORTING MIRROR* and with this number we complete the year which is generally so hazardous and so disastrous to the majority of new literary ventures. Happily, from our launch we have been fortunate enough to steer clear of all the rocks and quicksand in the sea of failure, and have guided our ship safely to its harbour once more after a most successful twelve months voyage."

"During that period we have been constantly on the lookout; constantly on the alert, for every opportunity to improve and extend the position of this magazine. Results prove that our endeavours have not been made in vain. From the launch our progress has been sure and steady. 'Onward' has been our motto and up to the present our success has far exceeded our most sanguine expectations."

"In embarking on another year of work we do so with our original confidence considerably strengthened and now that *THE SPORTING MIRROR* has secured a firm position in the literature of this country no laxity on our part will cause it to diminish in popularity. Our readers are, perhaps, the best judges whether we have fulfilled the mission on which we embarked; whether we have retained their confidence to the same extent we originally possessed, but on our side the success causes us to feel certain that the position has been firmly secured."

"With regard to our intentions in the future we intend to continue in the same groove and on the same road on which we have travelled up to the present. Of course, with the march of time improvements will necessarily follow, and we rightly anticipate making the same headway that we have done in the past. As a medium for advertisers we now rank second to none and the rewards we have received fully prove that our efforts in this quarter have been appreciated."

"Each month shows that our connection is rapidly spreading; our circulation is increasing, and we are now not only found in the libraries of English homes but sportsmen in America and on the far away continent of Australia are included in our clientele. In conclusion we must heartily thank those many friends who have interested themselves so greatly in our behalf during our early days and hope that they will still accord us the helping hand for which we feel so thoroughly grateful."

*   *   *   *   *

It seems no time at all since my first title was published. Alas, that was way back in 1968 and since that time I have been scribbling on a regular basis. This is now my sixtieth book and in some respects it has been one of the most interesting.

As has been mentioned on the Acknowledgements pages of previous titles I would like to pay my deepest thanks to Aled Jones at the National Library of Wales in Aberystwyth for his ability to find detail which had often drawn a blank for me. Also thanks to Paul Morgan, Greg Way, Ken Callahan, John Turton and Emma Morris who all, in their own way, gave me guidance and assistance.

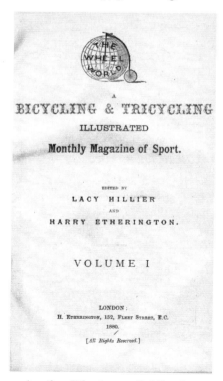

Another Etherington Publication

ISSUES

(Volumes 1 to 10, 1881-86, 60 issues)

1	Issue 1 - February 1881	(p1-32)
	Issue 2 - March 1881	(p33-64)
	Issue 3 - April 1881	(p65-104)
	Issue 4 - May 1881	(p105-144)
	Issue 5 - June 1881	(p145-184)
	Issue 6 - July 1881	(p185-224)
2	Issue 7 - August 1881	(p1-36)
	Issue 8 - September 1881	(p37-76)
	Issue 9 - October 1881	(p77-116)
	Issue 10 - November 1881	(p117-156)
	Issue 11 - December 1881	(p157-196)
	Issue 12 - January 1882	(p197-232)
3	Issue 13 - February 1882	(p1-56)
	Issue 14 - March 1882	(p57-104)
	Issue 15 - April 1882	(p105-152)
	Issue 16 - May 1882	(p153-200)
	Issue 17 - June 1882	(p201-248)
	Issue 18 - July 1882	(p249-292)
4	Issue 19 - August 1882	(p1-48)
	Issue 20 - September 1882	(p49-96)
	Issue 21 - October 1882	(p97-144)
	Issue 22 - November 1882	(p145-192)
	Issue 23 - December 1882	(p193-240)
	Issue 24 - January 1883	(p241-284)
5	Issue 25 - February 1883	(p1-56)
	Issue 26 - March 1883	(p57-112)
	Issue 27 - April 1883	(p113-160)
	Issue 28 - May 1883	(p161-208)
	Issue 29 - June 1883	(p209-256)
	Issue 30 - July 1883	(p257-300)

6	Issue 31 - August 1883	(p1-48)
	Issue 32 - September 1883	(p49-96)
	Issue 33 - October 1883	(p97-144)
	Issue 34 - November 1883	(p145-192)
	Issue 35 - December 1883	(p193-240)
	Issue 36 - January 1884	(p241-288)
7	Issue 37 - February 1884	(p1-48)
	Issue 38 - March 1884	(p49-104)
	Issue 39 - April 1884	(p105-160)
	Issue 40 - May 1884	(p161-208)
	Issue 41 - June 1884	(p209-256)
	Issue 42 - July 1884	(p257-300)
8	Issue 43 - August 1884	(p1-48)
	Issue 44 - September 1884	(p49-96)
	Issue 45 - October 1884	(p97-144)
	Issue 46 - November 1884	(p145-192)
	Issue 47 - December 1884	(p193-240)
	Issue 48 - January 1885	(p241-284)
9	Issue 49 - February 1885	(p1-48)
	Issue 50 - March 1885	(p49-96)
	Issue 51 - April 1885	(p97-144)
	Issue 52 - May 1885	(p145-192)
	Issue 53 - June 1885	(p193-240)
	Issue 54 - July 1885	(p241-284)
10	Issue 55 - August 1885	(p1-48)
	Issue 56 - September 1885	(p49-96)
	Issue 57 - October 1885	(p97-144)
	Issue 58 - November 1885	(p145-192)
	Issue 59 - December 1885	(p193-240)
	Issue 60 - January 1886	(p241-284)

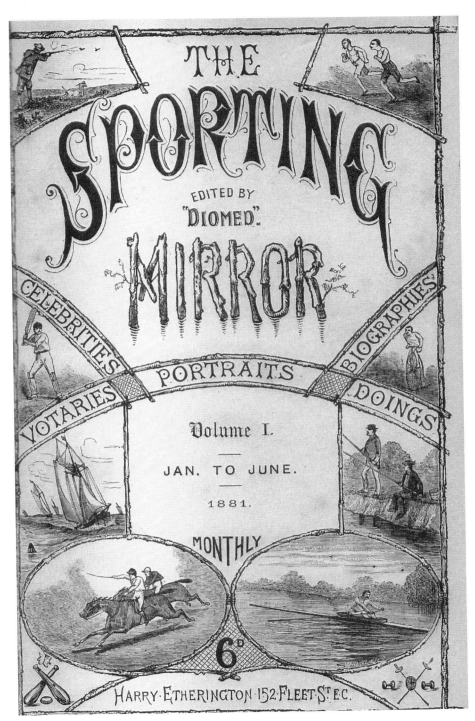

THE SPORTING MIRROR

EDITED BY "DIOMED".

CELEBRITIES · PORTRAITS · BIOGRAPHIES

VOTARIES · DOINGS

Volume I.

JAN. TO JUNE.

1881.

MONTHLY

6d.

HARRY · ETHERINGTON · 152 · FLEET · St · EC.

INDEX.

ARTICLES—   PAGE

Amateurs and Professionals 163
Athletic Diplomacy 191
Among the Blades 81
Backing Horses 150
Diamond cut Diamond 159
Eccentric Character, An 206
Evening Sprint, An 124
Gentlemen Amateurs 79
Guildford Coach, The 204
Lacrosse Laudation, A 119
Lunch, A Shooting 57
Pot-Hunting 122
Rearing Game 86
Rook Shooting 166
Saddle and Paddock 204
Trout of the Thames, The 111

BIOGRAPHIES AND PORTRAITS—

Archer, Fred 108
Astley, Sir John Dugdale 3
Blake, Charles (" Augur ") 105
Beresford, Lord Marcus 186
Constable, Henry 33
Cortis, Herbert Liddell 12
Cooper, Frederick 44
Davenport, Horace 113
George, W. G. 156
Grace, William Gilbert 37
Grace, George Frederick 157
Hanlan, Edward 8
Lockton, Charles Langton 40
Mitchell, John (" Vigilant ") 148
Myers, Eugene Laurence 196

16

Reay, J. H. A. 113

Rosebery, Lord 65

Ross, Wallace 68

Rous, Admiral 145

Rowell, Charles 16

Sampson, Henry (" Pendragon ") 72

Smith, R. Frost 76

Smurthwaite, Henry (" Bleys ") 188

Vize, George Henry 193

CHRONOLOGY—

January 31

February 61

March 99

April 140

May 179

June 219

POEMS—

Brook, The 121

Chase, The 75

Our Parson 107

Pretty Little Woman 165

Race, The 152

REFLECTIONS—

Athletics 25, 51, 96, 136, 173, 215

Aquatics 23, 50, 134, 178, 216

Australian Notes 30

Bicycling 52, 94, 138, 177

Billiards 24

Boxing 96, 135

Cricket 131, 176, 217

Coursing 23, 48, 93

Dramatic 54, 97, 127, 208

Pigeon Shooting 50

Skating 28

Turfiana 20, 46, 90, 129, 169, 210

John Astley

Edward Hanlan

Herbert Cortis

Charles Rowell

Volume One

February - July 1881

Issue 1 : February 1881

Portrait of John Astley	(facing p1)
Introduction	(p1-2)
Biography - John Astley [The Turf] by HBB	(p3-7)
Biography - Edward Hanlan [Sculling] by HBB	(p8-11)
Portrait of Edward Hanlan	(facing p8)
Biography - Herbert Cortis [Cycling] by HBB	(p12-15)
Portrait of Herbert Cortis	(facing p12)
Biography - Charles Rowell [Pedestrianism] by HBB	(p16-19)
Portrait of Charles Rowell	(facing p16)
January Reflections :	
Turfiana	(p20-22)
Coursing	(p23)
Aquatics	(p23-24)
Billiards	(p24-25)
Athletics	(p25-28)
Skating	(p28-29)
Australian Notes	(p30)
Sporting Chronology - January 1881	(p31-32)

Issue 2 : March 1881

Portrait of Henry Constable	(facing p33)
Biography - Henry Constable [Jockey] by HBB	(p33-36)
Portrait of Gilbert Grace	(facing p37)
Biography - Gilbert Grace [Cricket] by HBB	(p37-39)
Biography - Charles Lockton [Athletics] by HBB	(p40-43)
Portrait of Charles Lockton	(facing p40)
Biography - Frederick Cooper [Cycling] by HBB	(p44-45)
Portrait of Frederick Cooper	(facing p44)
February Reflections :	
Turfiana	(p46-48)
Coursing	(p48-49)
Pigeon Shooting	(p50)
Aquatics	(p50-51)
Athletics	(p51)

Henry Constable

Gilbert Grace

Charles Lockton

Frederick Cooper

Bicycling	(p52-53)
Dramatic Reflections	(p54-56)
A Shooting Lunch [Fiction] by Turley Mainprise	(p57-60)
Sporting Chronology - February 1881	(p61-64)

[William Turley Mainprise obtained his degree at the University of London in 1865 and was subsequently employed at the Admiralty. He was then a student of the Middle Temple until called to the bar in April 1869. Later he became a professional writer contributing to numerous magazines over a forty year period]

Issue 3 : April 1881

Portrait of Archibald Rosebery (Lord Rosebery)	(facing p65)
Biography - Archibald Rosebery [The Turf] by HBB	(p65-67)
Biography - Wallace Ross [Sculling] by HBB	(p68-71)
Portrait of Wallace Ros	(facing p68)
Biography - Henry Sampson [Sporting Journalist] by HBB	(p72-74)
Portrait of Henry Sampson	(facing p72)
The Chase [verses] by Mowbray Malonek	(p75)
Biography - Robert Frost-Smith [Boxing] by HBB	(p76-78)
Portrait of Robert Frost-Smith	(facing p76)
Gentleman Amateurs by HBB	(p79-80)
Among the Blades [Fiction] by Louis Clements	(p81-86)
Rearing Game by James Bertram	(p86-89)
March Reflections :	
Turfiana	(p90-92)
Coursing	(p93-94)
Bicycling	(p94-96)
Athletics	(p96)
Boxing	(p96)
Dramatic Reflections	(p97-98)
Sporting Chronology - March 1881	(p99-104)

[Mowbray George Malonek was born in Bideford, Devon and educated at the United Services College. He became good friends with the author and journalist Sir Home Gordon who employed him to write parts of the *Encyclopedia Britannica*. He also worked for the Gordon owned publishing house of Williams & Norgate. On Gordon's death, Malonek inherited his businesses and estates]

Archibald Rosebery

Wallace Ross

Henry Sampson

Robert Frost-Smith

Issue 4 : May 1881

Portrait of Charles Blake (facing p105)
Biography - Charles Blake [Sporting Journalist] by HBB (p105-107)
Our Parson [verses] by Mowbray Malonek (p107)
Biography - Fred Archer [Jockey] by HBB (p108-110)
Portrait of Fred Archer (facing p108)
The Trout of the Thames by John Keene (p111-112)
Portrait of Jack Reay (facing p113)
Biography - Jack Reay [Athletics] by HBB (p113-115)
Biography - Horace Davenport [Swimming] by HBB (p116-118)
Portrait of Horace Davenport (facing p116)
A Lacrosse Laudation [Montreal Lacrosse Club] (p119-121)
The Brook [verses] by Mowbray Malonek (p121)
Pot Hunting by HBB (p122-123)
An Evening Sprint [Fiction] (p124-126)
Dramatic Reflections (p127-128)
April Reflections :
    Turfiana (p129-131)
    Cricket (p131-133)
    Aquatics (p134)
    Boxing (p135-136)
    Athletics (p136-138)
    Bicycling (p138-139)
Sporting Chronology - April 1881 (p140-144)

[John Harrington Keene was a prolific author on all matters concerning angling. He was born in Weybridge,Surrey in 1855 and was first published at sixteen years of age. He emigrated to America in 1885 on the death of his father. He prospered for many years but illness saw him slide into poverty. He died in Vermont in 1907]

Issue 5 : June 1881

Portrait of Henry Rous (facing p145)
Biography - Henry Rous [The Turf] by HBB (p145-147)
Biography - Jack Mitchell [Sporting Journalist] by HBB (p148-149)
Portrait of Jack Mitchell (facing p148)
Backing Horses by Martin Cobbett (p150-152)
The Race [verses] by Mowbray Malonek (p152)
Portrait of Walter George (facing p153)

Charles Blake

Fred Archer

Jack Reay

Horace Davenport

Biography - Walter George [Athletics] by HBB	(p153-156)
Portrait of Frederick Grace	(facing p157)
Biography - Frederick Grace [Cricket] by HBB	(p157-158)
Diamond Cut Diamond [Fiction] by HBB	(p159-162)
Amateurs and Professionals by HBB	(p163-165)
A Pretty Little Woman [verses] by Mowbray Malonek	(p165)
Rook Shooting by HBB	(p166-168)
May Reflections :	
Turfiana	(p169-173)
Athletics	(p173-176)
Cricket	(p176-177)
Bicycling	(p177-178)
Aquatics	(p178)
Sporting Chronology - May 1881	(p179-184)

Issue 6 : July 1881

Portrait of Marcus Beresford (Lord Beresford)	(facing p185)
Biography - Marcus Beresford [The Turf] by HBB	(p185-187)
Biography - Henry Smurthwaite [Sporting Journalist] by HBB	(p188-190)
Portrait of Henry Smurthwaite	(facing p188)
Athletic Diplomacy by Martin Cobbett	(p191-192)
Portrait of George Vize	(facing p193)
Biography - George Vize [Athletics] by HBB	(p193-195)
Biography - Laurence Myers [Athletics] by HBB	(p196-199)
Portrait of Laurence Myers	(facing p196)
Saddle and Paddock by HBB	(p200-203)
The Guildford Coach by Stanley Harris	(p204-206)
An Eccentric Character by Stanley Harris	(p206-207)
Dramatic Reflections	(p208-209)
June Reflections :	
Turfiana	(p210-215)
Athletics	(p215-216)
Aquatics	(p216)
Cricket	(p217-218)
Military Tournament Exhibits	(p218)
Sporting Chronology - June 1881	(p219-224)

[Stanley Harris was the author of *Old Coaching Days* and *The Coaching Age*, both of which are considered to be definitive histories. He commented about "the golden age of coaching" which, he says, "reached a state of perfection from 1820-40"]

Henry Rous

Jack Mitchell

Walter George

Fred Grace

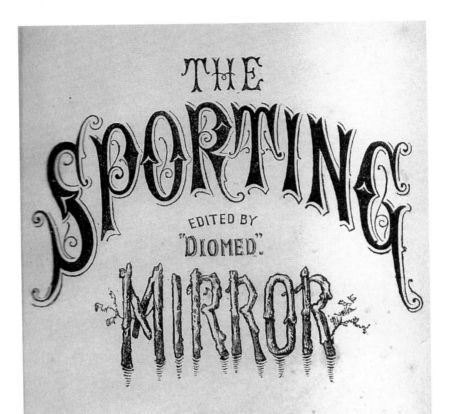

THE SPORTING MIRROR

EDITED BY "DIOMED".

CELEBRITIES, VOTARIES, PORTRAITS,
BIOGRAPHIES, DOINGS.

Volume II.

JULY TO DECEMBER.

1881.

HARRY ETHERINGTON, 152, Fleet Street, London, E.C.

Marcus Beresford

Henry Smurthwaite

George Vize

Laurence Myers

INDEX.

ARTICLES—   PAGE
  Aquatic Reminiscence, An   212
  Bicycle Union an Error? Is the   137
    ,,   ,,   ,,   A Reply...   ...   177
  Buffalo Hunting with Dr. Carver   215
  Century of Pedestrianism   142
  Country Houses   3
  Cover Side, At the   134
  Cricket Chat, A   55
  Cricket in 1881...   101
  Curling   199
  Day, Sen., A Chat about John   119
  England v. America   14
  English and American Timing   47
  Forestalling   174
  Fishing in the Fens   51
  Fishing with a "Trowle"   219
  Football Season, The Coming   98
  Grouse Shooting   17
  Hunting Reminiscences   139
  Perch, Amongst the   97
  Pheasant Shooting   83
  Pike Fishing in the Welland...   20
  "Sir Tatton's," The Two   180
  Sport with the Harriers   171
  Sportsman's Exhibition 167, 203
  Sport in Boston Deeps   93
  Trotting   58
  Trout Tickling...   127
  Turnips, In the   60

BIOGRAPHIES AND PORTRAITS—

  Ashley, Mr. Charles Hitchin (Sportsman)   117
  Atkinson, Mr. George William (Sporting Life) ...   49
  Cannon, Tom   77
  Carver, Dr. W. F.   158
  Cowie, Mr. J. Milroy...   205
  Crute, Mr. Charles   89

BIOGRAPHIES AND PORTRAITS (*continued*)—   PAGE

    Daft, Richard 121
    Donnelly, Ned 169
    Fordham, George 37
    Goodlake, V.C., Major-General Gerald 197
    Hillier, Mr. George Lacy 44
    Hulton, Mr. Edward (*Manchester Sporting Chronicle*) 201
    Laycock, Elias 80
    Leverell, Mr. W. H. (*Bell's Life*) 165
    Lowndes, Mr. Jefferson 209
    Macdonald, William (the Late) 161
    Mason, Mr. Charles H. 129
    Merrill, E. E. 5
    Oliver, Mr. H. M. (*Midland Athlete*) 9
    Phillips, Mr. W. Page 85
    Trickett, Edward 41
    Webster, Mr. James 12
    Whitefoot, Mr. Tom B. (*Sportsman*) 1
    Wood, Charles 125

CHRONOLOGY—

    July 31
    August 72
    September 113
    October 154
    November 193
    December 228

POEMS—

    Coming Season, The 97
    Hunting Song 173
    Opening Day, The 133
    Past and Present 11
    Poem for Piscators, A 208

REFLECTIONS—

    Aquatics 70, 189, 226
    Athletics 69
    Bicycling 70, 152
    Dramatic 25, 63, 106, 146, 183, 221
    Football 153, 190, 227
    Turfiana 27, 65, 108, 148, 185, 223

REVIEWS 191

Volume Two

August 1881 - January 1882

Issue 7 : August 1881

Portrait of Thomas Whitefoot	(facing p1)
Biography - Thomas Whitefoot [Sporting Journalist] by HBB	(p1-2)
Country Houses by HBB	(p3-4)
Portrait of Edward Merrill	(facing p5)
Biography - Edward Merrill [Athletics] by HBB	(p5-8)
Portrait of Harry Oliver	(facing p9)
Biography - Harry Oliver [Athletics/Journalist] by HBB	(p9-11)
Past and Present [verses] by Mowbray Malonek	(p11)
Biography - James Webster [The Turf] by HBB	(p12-13)
Portrait of James Webster	(facing p12)
England versus America [Athletics Meeting] by HBB	(p14-17)
Grouse Shooting by William Lamonby	(p17-20)
Pike Fishing in the Welland by HBB	(p20-24)
Dramatic Reflections	(p25-26)
July Reflections : Turfiana	(p27-30)
Sporting Chronology - July 1881	(p31-36)

[William Lamonby started his journalism career in Australia and spent most of his working life as the coursing and falconry writer of *The Field*. His accuracy in anything he did was unquestionable. He also wrote on football, cricket and athletics. He died in 1925]

Issue 8 : September 1881

Portrait of George Fordham	(facing p37)
Biography - George Fordham [Jockey] by HBB	(p37-40)
Portrait of Edward Trickett	(facing p41)
Biography - Edward Trickett [Sculling] by HBB	(p41-43)
Biography - George Hillier [Cycling] by HBB	(p44-46)
Portrait of George Hillier	(facing p44)
English versus American Timing by HBB	(p47-48)
Portrait of George Atkinson	(facing p49)
Biography - George Atkinson [Sporting Journalist] by HBB	(p49-50)
Fishing in the Fens by Wilfrid Pocklington	(p51-53)
A Cricket Chat by HBB	(p54-57)

Thomas Whitefoot

Edward Merrill

Harry Oliver

James Webster

Trotting by HBB   (p58-59)
In the Turnips [Partridge Shooting] by HBB   (p60-62)
Dramatic Reflections   (p63-64)
August Reflections :
    Turfiana   (p65-68)
    Athletics   (p68-70)
    Aquatics   (p70)
    Bicycling   (p70-71)
Sporting Chronology - August 1881   (p72-76)
Hedozone Table Water   (p76)

Issue 9 : October 1881

Portrait of Thomas Cannon   (facing p77)
Biography - Thomas Cannon [Jockey] by HBB   (p77-79)
Biography - Elias Laycock [Sculling] by HBB   (p80-82)
Portrait of Elias Laycock   (facing p80)
Pheasant Shooting by William Lamonby   (p83-84)
Portrait of Page Phillips   (facing p85)
Biography - Page Phillips [Athletics] by HBB   (p85-88)
Portrait of Charles Crute   (facing p89)
Biography - Charles Crute [Cycling] by HBB   (p89-92)
Sport in Boston Deeps by Wilfrid Pocklington   (p93-95)
Amongst the Perch by John Keene   (p96-97)
The Coming Season [verses] by Mowbray Malonek   (p97)
The Coming [Association & Rugby] Football Season by HBB (p98-100)
Cricket in 1881 by Rowland Hill   (p101-105)
Dramatic Reflections   (p106-107)
September Reflections :
    Turfiana   (p108-112)
    Post Horns   (p112)
    Eclipse Boot   (p112)
Sporting Chronology - September 1881   (p113-116)

[George Rowland Hill (1855-1928) was, for many years, both secretary and president of the Rugby Football Union. He wrote for and edited numerous books including *Football: The Rugby Union Game* (with Fred Marshall); *Modern Football* (with Charles Marriott) and *Famous Footballers* (with Charles Alcock)]

George Fordham

Edward Trickett

George Hillier

George Atkinson

Issue 10 : November 1881

Portrait of Charles Ashley .... (facing p117)
Biography - Charles Ashley [Sporting Journalist] by HBB .... (p117-118)
A Chat About John Day by William Lamonby .... (p119-120)
Portrait of Richard Daft .... (facing p121)
Biography - Richard Daft [Cricketer] by HBB .... (p121-124)
Portrait of Charles Wood .... (facing p125)
Biography - Charles Wood [Jockey] by HBB .... (p125-126)
Trout Tickling by John Keene .... (p127-128)
Harness against Time .... (p128)
Pedestrian Feat of 1795 .... (p128)
Portrait of Charles Mason .... (facing p129)
Biography - Charles Mason [Athletics] by HBB .... (p129-132)
The Opening Day [verses] by Mowbray Malonek .... (p133)
At the Cover Side [Hunting] by HBB .... (p134-136)
Is The Bicycle Union an Error by Harry Etherington .... (p137-138)
Hunting Reminiscences by Wilfrid Pocklington .... (p139-141)
A Sporting Eccentric - James Hirst .... (p141)
A Century of Pedestrianism by HBB .... (p142-145)
Sam Chifney - Jockey .... (p145)
James Croft - Horse Trainer .... (p145)
Singular Accident to a Horse while Running .... (p145)
Dramatic Reflections .... (p146-147)
October Reflections :
    Turfiana .... (p148-151)
    Bicycling .... (p152-153)
    Rugby Football Union - Annual General Meeting ... (p153)
Sporting Chronology - October 1881 .... (p154-156)

Issue 11 : December 1881

Portrait of Frank Carver .... (facing p157)
Biography - Frank Carver [Shooting] by HBB .... (p157-160)
Portrait of William Macdonald .... (facing p161)
Biography - William Macdonald [Jockey] by HBB .... (p161-164)
Portrait of Harry Leverell .... (facing p165)
Biography - Harry Leverell [Sporting Journalist] by HBB .... (p165-166)
The Sportsman's Exhibition by HBB .... (p167-168)
Warned off Newmarket Heath .... (p168)
Portrait of Ned Donnelly .... (facing p169)

Thomas Cannon

Elias Laycock

Page Phillips

Charles Crute

Biography - Ned Donnelly [Boxing] by HBB (p169-170)
Sport With the Harriers by Wilfrid Pocklington (p171-173)
Hunting Song [verses] by Mowbray Malonek (p173)
Forestalling [Fiction] (p174-176)
Hambletonian and Diamond at Newmarket (p176)
The Deerfoot of 1788 (p176)
Is The Bicycle Union An Error - A Reply (p177-179)
The Two Sir Tatton's by HBB (p180-182)
Captain Barclay Allardice's Death (p182)
Dramatic Reflections (p183-184)
November Reflections :
    Turfiana (p185-189)
    Aquatics (p189-190)
    Football Association Challenge Cup (p190-191)
Book Reviews
    The Gun and its Development by William Greener (p191-192)
    Lawn Tennis: Its Players & How to Play by Robert Osborn (p192)
    Ludgate Hill: Past and Present by William Treloar (p192)
Sporting Chronology - October / November 1881 (p193-196)

Issue 12 : January 1882

Portrait of Gerald Goodlake (facing p197)
Biography - Gerald Goodlake [Sportsman] by HBB (p197-198)
Curling by HBB (p199-200)
Portrait of Edward Hulton (facing p201)
Biography - Edward Hulton [Sporting Journalist] by HBB (p201-202)
The Sportsman's Exhibition by HBB (p203-204)
Captain Barclay Allardice's First Feat (p204)
Bill Scott's St.Leger Victories (p204)
Portrait of Jefferson Lowndes (facing p205)
Biography - Jefferson Lowndes [Sculling] by HBB (p205-207)
A Poem for Piscators [verses] by Henry Newton (p208)
Portrait of Milroy Cowie (facing p209)
Biography - Milroy Cowie [Athletics] by HBB (p209-211)
An Aquatic Reminiscence [Fiction] by Wilfrid Pocklington (p212-214)
The Two Popes [Horses] (p214)
Tommy Nicholson and the St.Leger of 1831 (p214)
Pocahontas [Horse] (p214)
Buffalo Hunting with Frank Carver by William Lamonby (p215-218)
Twenty-Three Miles in the Hour (p218)

Charles Ashley

Richard Daft

Charles Wood

Charles Mason

The Owner of Eclipse — (p218)
Fishing With a Trowle by John Keene — (p219-220)
Dramatic Reflections — (p221-222)
December Reflections :
    Turfiana — (p223-226)
    Aquatics — (p226-227)
    Rugby Football Union — (p227-228)
To Our Readers [Resume of First Year of Publication] — (p228)
Sporting Chronology - November / December 1881 — (p229-232)
Royal Agricultural Society Journal [Chaff-Cutters] — (p232)

[Henry Chance Newton (1854-1931) was an author, journalist and critic. He started on *Hood's Comic Annual* in 1875; was the London correspondent for *The New York Dramatic Mirror*; then moved to *The Referee*. He also wrote libretti for musical comedy]

Lancaster & Co.

Frank Carver

William Macdonald

Harry Leverell

Ned Donnelly

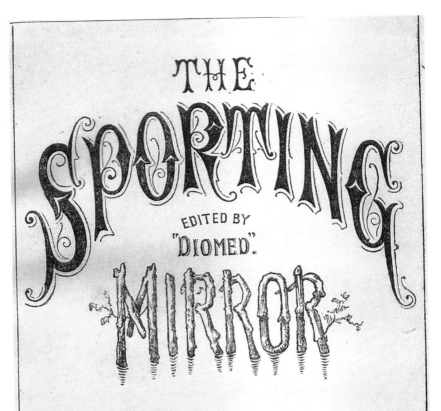

THE SPORTING MIRROR

EDITED BY "DIOMED".

CELEBRITIES, VOTARIES, PORTRAITS, BIOGRAPHIES, DOINGS.

Volume III.

JANUARY TO JUNE.

1882.

HARRY ETHERINGTON, 152, Fleet Street, London, E.C.

Gerald Goodlake

Edward Hulton

Jefferson Lowndes

Milroy Cowie

INDEX.

ARTICLES— PAGE

Athletic Abuses and the Remedies. By Trechon ... 62
Baulk Match at Pigeons, A. By One who has Fired
   20,000 Shots at Marks 175
"Bound to Go." By Hal Lowther 277
Broken Down. By Austin Moray 144
Canadian Cedar-rib Canoe 25
Carholme Reminiscence, A. By Argus-Eye 139
Chat about Squire Osbaldeston, A. By Helvellyn ... 10
Chat about John Gully, A. By Helvellyn 122
Coaching Season, The. By W. A. 181
Coaching Season in May, The. By Waller Ashe ... 249
Coursing in the Fens. By Wilf. Pocklington... ... 31
"Down the Road." By Waller Ashe 281
Edinburgh Fisheries Exhibition, The 188
English and American Thoroughbreds. By H. B.
   Bromhead 127
Football—Its Past and Possible Development. By
   Arthur Budd 140
How to Choose a Gun. By One who has Fired 20,000
   Shots at Marks 226
How to Load a Gun. By One who has Fired 20,000
   Shots at Marks... 271
Last Day of the Season, The (hunting). By Austin
   Moray 236
London Holiday, A. By J. P. Wheeldon 193
Lucky Fall, A. By Austin Moray 17
Modern Gunpowders. By One who has Fired 20,000
   Shots at Marks... 138
My First Salmon. By Austin Moray 185
Parson's Mare, The. By Austin Moray 98
Pike Fishing. By J. P. Wheeldon 27
Punchestown; or, My Winning Mount. By Waller Ashe 89
Reminiscences of Jem Mace. By Hal Lowther ... 232
Rowing—Retrospective and Prospective. By W. H.
   Leverell 120
Some Irish Sport. By Austin Moray 68
Some Old Shooting Matches. By H. B. B. 251
Some Future Cricket. By H. B. Bromhead 190
Spinning for Thames Trout. By J. P. Wheeldon ... 137
Sport v. Sportsmen. By Finch Mason 33
Sporting Contrasts. By J. P. Wheeldon 214
Sportsman's Exhibition, The. By Diomed 19, 75
Skating and Skaters. By H. B. Bromhead 23
The Australian Cricket Averages 270
The Opening Day on the Thames. By J. P. Wheeldon 266
Wild Fowling. By Tintagel 36
Woodcock Shooting in Syria. By Wanderer 101

PORTRAITS AND BIOGRAPHIES—   PAGE.

Beaufort, The Duke of 57
Barron, Hunter Jackson 165
Bligh, Hon. Ivo Francis Walter 205
Bonnor, George John 263
Boyd, Robert Watson 115
Cook, William 13
Custance, Henry 161
Day, John 65
Giffen, George 265
Hanlan, Edward 113
Hardaway, Jack 118
Holman, S. K. 169
Hornby, Mr. Albert Neilson 5
Jackson, M.A., Clement Nugent 253
Jones, S. P. 264
Murdoch, William Lloyd 257
Osborne, John 109
Pennell, Mr. H. Cholmondeley- 9
Portland, The Duke of 1
Richardson, John Maunsell 109
Richmond, The Duke of 249
Ross, Captain Horatio 154
Shaw, Alfred 69
Spofforth, Frederick Robert 261
Turner-Turner, Mr. J. 61
Valentine, George 117
Westminster, The Duke of 201
Wilton, (The Late) Earl of 106
Wise, Bernhard Ringrose 217

POEMS—

A Cricketing Carol. By H. C. Newton 260
A "Sound" Sportsman. By H. C. Newton 4
Ballad of the Blues, A. By H. C. Newton 148
Bang-tailed Mare. By M. G. M. 187
Gone Away. By M. G. M. 32
March Meditation, A. By H. C. Newton 97
May Mems. By H. C. Newton 160
Old Inn, The. By Harry Beecher 126
Twelve-Bores *v* Ten-Bores. By Sandy Ridge 222
Waltonian Warble, A. By H. C. Newton 208

OUR GUNMAKERS—

Lancaster, Charles 21
Needham, Mr. J. V. 221
Purdey, James and Sons 73
Rigby, John and Co. 125
Silver, S. W., and Co. 169
Westley Richards and Co. 173

REFLECTIONS—

Aquatics. By Diomed 47, 248
Dramatic. By Conn 39, 71, 149, 197, 223, 285
Coursing. By Diomed 46
Turfiana. By Diomed 42, 103, 151, 199, 242, 287

Volume Three

February - July 1882

Issue 13 : February 1882

Portrait of William Cavendish-Bentinck (Duke of Portland)	(facing p1)
Biography - William Cavendish-Bentinck [The Turf] by HBB	(p1-3)
A Sound Sportsman [verses] by Henry Newton	(p4)
Portrait of Albert Hornby	(facing p5)
Biography - Albert Hornby [Cricketer] by HBB	(p5-8)
Portrait of Henry Cholmondeley-Pennell	(facing p9)
Biography - Henry Cholmondeley-Pennell [Fishing] by HBB	(p9)
A Chat About Squire Osbaldeston by William Lamonby	(p10-12)
Portrait of William Cook	(facing p13)
Biography - William Cook [Billiards] by HBB	(p13-16)
A Lucky Fall [Fiction] by Austin Moray	(p17-20)
Doncaster Races	(p20)
Lithograph of Four-Barrelled Hammerless Gun	(facing p21)
Our Gunmakers - Charles Lancaster by HBB	(p21-22)
Skating and Skaters by HBB	(p23-24)
Lithograph of Canadian Cedar-Rib Canoe	(facing p25)
The Canadian Cedar-Rib Canoe by HBB	(p25-26)
Pike Fishing by Joseph Wheeldon	(p27-29)
An Ancient Sportsman - Squire Mellish	(p29)
Coursing in the Fens [Fiction] by Wilfrid Pocklington	(p30-32)
Gone Away [verses] by Mowbray Malonek	(p32)
Sport and Sportsmen by Finch Mason	(p33-35)
Wild-Fowling by HBB	(p36-38)
Ancient Newmarket	(p38)
Matchmaking [Horses]	(p38)
Death of Captain Barclay-Allardice in 1854	(p38)
Dramatic Reflections	(p39-41)
January Reflections :	
Turfiana	(p42-45)
Coursing	(p46-47)
Aquatics	(p47-48)
The Sportsman's Exhibition by HBB	(p49-56)

[George Finch Mason was educated at Eton and being fond of all outdoor sports he soon turned his hand to writing. He had numerous books published and was

William Cavendish-Bentinck

Albert Hornby

Henry Cholmondeley-Pennell

William Cook

the only editor of *The Badminton Magazine of Sports and Pastimes*. He died as he completed the January 1923 issue. His autobiography was titled *A Sporting and Dramatic Career*]

Issue 14 : March 1882

Portrait of Henry Somerset (Duke of Beaufort	(facing p57)
Biography - Henry Somerset [The Turf] by HBB	(p57-60)
Portrait of John Turner-Turner	(facing p61)
Biography - John Turner-Turner [Shooting] by HBB	(p61)
Athletic Abuses and their Remedies by Thomas Sutton	(p62-64)
Portrait of John Day	(facing p65)
Biography - John Day [The Turf] by HBB	(p65)
Some Irish Sport [Fiction] by Austin Moray	(p66-68)
Portrait of Alfred Shaw	(facing p69)
Biography - Alfred Shaw [Cricketer] by HBB	(p69-70)
Dramatic Reflections	(p71-72)
Lithograph of Rebounding Hammerless Gun	(facing p73)
Our Gunmakers - James Purdy by HBB	(p73-74)
Pedestrian Profits	(p74)
Samuel Kitchener, Jockey	(p74)
The Sportsman's Exhibition by HBB	(p75-88)
Cigarette Smoking - Richmond Gems	(p88)
Punchestown or My Winning Mount [Fiction] by Waller Ashe	(p89-96)
A March Meditation [verses] by Henry Newton	(p97)
The Parson's Mare [Fiction] by Hal Burghley	(p98-100)
Woodcock Shooting in Syria by William Scarth-Dixon	(p101-103)
February Reflections : Turfiana	(p103-104)

[William Scarth-Dixon (1848-1933) was an agriculturist, hunting man and a participant in every kind of sport. In the early 1880s his writing career took priority and he contributed regularly to *The Country Gentleman* and to *The Field*. He also wrote numerous sporting books]

Purdey & Sons

Henry Somerset

John Turner-Turner

John Day

Alfred Shaw

Issue 15 : April 1882

Portrait of Thomas Egerton (Earl of Wilton)	(facing p105)
Biography - Thomas Egerton [The Turf] by HBB	(p105-108)
Portrait of John Osborne	(facing p109)
Biography - John Osborne [Jockey] by HBB	(p109-112)
Portrait of Edward Hanlan	(facing p113)
Portrait of Robert Boyd	(facing p113)
Biography - Edward Hanlan [Sculling] by HBB	(p113-114)
Biography - Robert Boyd [Sculling] by HBB	(p115-116)
Portrait of George Hardaway	(facing p117)
Portrait of Jack Valentine	(facing p117)
Messrs Valentine and Hardaway [Bookmakers] by HBB	(p117-119)
Rowing: Retrospective and Prospective by William Leverell	(p120-121)
A Chat about John Gully by William Lamonby	(p122-124)
Book Reviews: *Sports & Pastimes* and *Indoor Amusements*	(p124)
Lithograph of an Improved Hammerless Gun	(facing p125)
Our Gunmakers - John Rigby by HBB	(p125-126)
The Old Inn [verses] by Harry Beecher	(p126)
English and American Thoroughbreds by HBB	(p127-130)
The Sportsman's Exhibition by HBB	(p130)
Modern Gunpowders by Arthur Lane	(p131-135)
Veil Protector	(p135)
Spinning for Thames Trout by Joseph Wheeldon	(p136-137)
A Carholme Reminiscence by Martin Cobbett	(p138-139)
[Rugby] Football: Past and Development by Arthur Budd	(p140-143)
India Rubber Pads for Horses' Shoes by Peter Martingale	(p143)
Broken Down [Fiction] by Austin Moray	(p144-147)
A Ballard of the Blues [verses] by Henry Newton	(p148)
Dramatic Reflections	(p149-150)
March Reflections : Turfiana	(p151-152)

Westley Richards & Co.'s
PATENT
HAMMERLESS GUN.

Richards & Co.

Thomas Egerton

John Osborne

Horatio Ross

Henry Custance

Issue 16 : May 1882

Portrait of Horatio Ross	(facing p153)
Biography - Horatio Ross [Shooting] by HBB	(p153-159)
May Mems [verses] by Henry Newton	(p160)
Portrait of Henry Custance	(facing p161)
Biography - Henry Custance [Jockey] by HBB	(p161-164)
Portrait of Hunter Barron	(facing p165)
Biography - Hunter Barron [Swimming] by HBB	(p165-168)
Portrait of Samuel Holman	(facing p169)
Biography - Samuel Holman [Athletics] by HBB	(p169-172)
Lithograph of a Hammerless Gun	(facing p173)
Our Gunmakers - Westley Richards by HBB	(p173-174)
Modern Gunpowders - Messrs Curtis & Harvey	(p174)
A Baulk Match at Pigeons [Fiction] by Arthur Lane	(p175-180)
A Cricketing Scrap - Women's Match 1801	(p180)
A Word about Caller Ou's St.Leger	(p180)
The Coaching Season by Waller Ashe	(p181-184)
Review of The Athletic Review edited by Edwin Sachs	(p184)
Canadian Cedar-Rib Canoe	(p184)
My First Salmon by Austin Moray	(p185-187)
The Bang-Tailed Mare [verses] by Mowbray Malonek	(p187)
The Edinburgh Fisheries Exhibition by HBB	(p188-189)
Patent Meat Fibrine Vegetable Dog Cakes (with Beetroot)	(p189)
Some Future Cricket by HBB	(p190-192)
A London Holiday by Joseph Wheeldon	(p193-196)
Morris's Dubecks Cigarettes and Roper Frere Champagne	(p196)
A Great Match: Mulberry against Sir Peter Teazle [Horses]	(p196)
Dramatic Reflections	(p197-198)
April Reflections : Turfiana	(p199-200)

[Waller Ashe was initially a military historian writing books such as *The Anglo-Zulu War of 1879; Records of the Kandahar Campaign* and *The Story of the Zulu Campaign*. Subsequently he wrote fiction and on many matters of sporting interest]

Issue 17 : June 1882

Portrait of Hugh Grosvenor (Duke of Westminster)	(facing p201)
Biography - Hugh Grosvenor [The Turf] by HBB	(p200-204)
Portrait of Ivo Bligh	(facing p205)

George Hardaway & Jack Valentine

Edward Hanlan & Robert Boyd

Biography - Ivo Bligh [Cricket] by HBB	(p205-207)
A Waltonian Warble [verses] by Henry Newton	(p208)
Portrait of John Maunsell-Richardson	(facing p209)
Biography - John Maunsell-Richardson [The Turf] by HBB	(p209-213)
Sporting Contrasts by Joseph Wheeldon	(p214-216)
Portrait of Bernhard Wise	(facing p217)
Biography - Bernhard Wise [Athletics] by HBB	(p217-220)
Lithograph of The Injector Hammerless Gun	(facing p221)
Our Gunmakers - Joseph Needham	(p221-222)
Twelve Bores versus Ten Bores [verses] by Sandy Ridge	(p222)
Luck Defeats Science - Trout Fishing Contest	(p222)
Dramatic Reflections	(p223-224)
Lithograph of an Outside Pillar Winch	(facing p225)
Mr Little's Outside Pillar Winch	(p225)
Tolly Gunmakers' Pioneer Works	(p225)
The Australian Cricketers	(p225)
How to Choose a Gun by Arthur Lane	(p226-231)
Reminiscences of Jim Mace by Hal Lowther	(p232-235)
Curious Facts - Lake Erie	(p235)
A Large Trout	(p235)
The Last Day of the Season by Austin Moray	(p236-238)
The Coaching Season in May by Waller Ashe	(p239-242)
Kincsem [Hungarian Horse]	(p242)
Voltigeur's Cat: Edwin Landseer's Picture	(p242)
Trout Frozen in a Block of Ice	(p242)
May Reflections :	
Turfiana	(p243-247)
Aquatics	(p248)

[Joseph Parker Wheeldon (1840-96) was for some years the angling correspondent of *Bell's Life*. He then joined *The Morning Advertiser* and also contributed to *The Sportsman*. His work also regularly appeared in *The Fishing Gazette*, *The Field* and *Land & Water*. He wrote a number of books]

Issue 18 : July 1882

Portrait of Charles Lennox (Duke of Richmond)	(facing p249)
Biography - Charles Lennox [The Turf] by HBB	(p249-250)
Some Old Shooting Matches by HBB	(p251-252)
Portrait of Clement Jackson	(facing p252)
Biography - Clement Jackson [Athletics] by HBB	(p253-256)

Hunter Barron

Samuel Holman

Hugh Grosvenor

Ivo Bligh

Portrait of William Murdoch (facing p257)
Biography - William Murdoch [Cricket] by HBB (p257-259)
A Cricketing Carol [verses] by Henry Newton (p260)
Portrait of Sammy Jones (facing p261)
Portrait of Frederick Spofforth (facing p261)
Biography - Frederick Spofforth [Cricket] by HBB (p261-262)
Biography - Sammy Jones [Cricket] by HBB (p263)
Biography - George Bonnor [Cricket] by HBB (p264)
Portrait of George Giffen (facing p264)
Portrait of George Bonnor (facing p264)
Biography - George Giffen [Cricket] by HBB (p265)
The Opening Day on the Thames by Joseph Wheeldon (p266-268)
Lithograph of a Hammerless Gun (facing p269)
Our Gunmakers - Samuel Silver by Arthur Lane (p269-270)
The Australian Cricket Averages (p270)
How to Load a Gun by Arthur Lane (p271-276)
Australian Cricketers Cabinet Photographs (p276)
Book Review: Training for Amateur Athletes by Herbert Cortis (p276)
Bound to Go [Fiction] by Hal Lowther (p277-280)
Down the Road by Waller Ashe (p281-284)
Dramatic Reflections (p285-286)
June Reflections : Turfiana (p287-292)

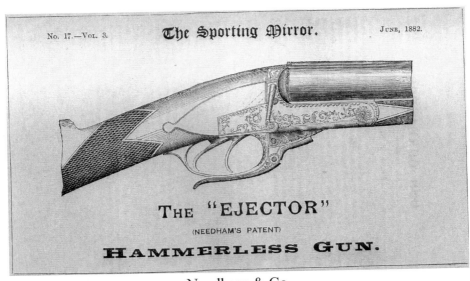

No. 17.—Vol. 3.   The Sporting Mirror.   JUNE, 1882.

THE "EJECTOR"

(NEEDHAM'S PATENT)

HAMMERLESS GUN.

Needham & Co.

John Maunsell Richardson

Bernhard Wise

Sammy Jones and Frederick Spofforth

George Giffen and George Bonnor

Charles Lennox

Clement Jackson

William Murdoch

Little & Co.

THE SPORTING MIRROR

EDITED BY "DIOMED".

CELEBRITIES, VOTARIES, PORTRAITS, BIOGRAPHIES, DOINGS.

Volume IV.

JULY TO DECEMBER.

1882.

HARRY ETHERINGTON, 152, Fleet Street, London, E.C.

Richard Boyle

Henry Ball

Jack Blackham

Alexander Bannerman

INDEX.

ARTICLES—   PAGE

A Very Queer Place. By J. P. Wheeldon   117
American Courtesy. By Argus-Eye   273
Birmingham Sportsman's Exhibition, The   130
Bit of Dubious Fishing, A. By J. P. Wheeldon   ...   161
Chat About the Chifneys, A. By Helvellyn   ...   144
Cottesmore Hunt, The. By Old Towler...   266
Cub Hunting Memories. By Diomed   131
Day's Spinning for Pike. By J. P. Wheeldon   ...   211
Deal—and a Sell, A. By Austin Moray   30
Elopement which Did Not Come Off. By One who has
      Fired 20,000 Shots, &c.   67
Equine Longevity. By Argus Eye   62
Fox-Hunting and Fox-Hunters. By Diomed   218
Gaur-Shooting in India. By Wanderer...   121
Gossip on Bream Fishing, A. By J. P. Wheeldon   ...   19
Hardwork of Racing, The. By H. B. Bromhead   ...   214
Horses' Feet, and How to Treat Them   224
How to Use a Gun. By One who has Fired, &c.   ...   30
Integrity of Racing, The. By H. B. Bromhead   ...   268
Jockeys' Mounts, 1882.   225
Lacrosse. By C. T. Sachs...   13
Miseries of Racing, The. By H. B. Bromhead   ...   11t
Not Out ; a Cricket Story. By John Dawson   79
Old Pedestrian Jottings. By Tintagel   74
Pike " Fishing " in Winter. By Wilfred Pocklington...   169
Pleasures of Racing, The. By H. B. Bromhead   ...   57
Robberies of Racing, The. By H. B. Bromhead   ...   172
Rod and Trigger—A Mixed Bag. By Diomed...   ...   262
Sailing, on a very Small Scale. By a Land Lubber   ...   83
Skating in the Fens. By Hal Forester   258
Snipe Shooting in the Fens. By Hal Forester...   ...   221
Some Peculiar Matches. By Helvellyn...   229
Sportsman's Exhibition 196, 261
Story of a Hunt, The. By Hal Lowther   176
With the Quorn at Kirby Gate. By Old Towler   ...   228

BIOGRAPHIES AND PORTRAITS—

Baker, Sidney Herbert   201
Ball, Henry Rawlins   4
Bannerman, Alexander Chambers   10
Beal, Charles William   56
Bennett, Joseph   205
Blackham, John McCarthy...   8
Boyle, Henry Frederick   60
Cork, The Earl of   1
Dudley-Ward, W. H.   101
Keith-Falconer, The Hon. Ion Grant Neville   49
Garrett, Thomas William   11
Gibb, James   105
Goater, James   53
Harris, Lord   241
Hartington, The Marquis of   97

BIOGRAPHIES AND PORTRAITS (*Continued*)—   PAGE

Horan, Thomas   12
Lane, Arthur James (One who has Fired 20,000 Shots
    at Marks)   197
Lennard, Sir Thomas Barrett   193
Massie, Hugh Hamon   108
McDonnell, Percy Stanislaus   61
Palmer, George Eugene   109
Peall, W. J.   253
Porter, John...   156
Roberts, W. John   149
Russell, The Rev. John   145
Savile, Mr. Henry, The Late   245
Sturt, Herbert Halse   153
Wood, Francis J. W.   249

OUR GUNMAKERS—

Bailey's Patent-Gastight Cartridges   64
Beattie and Co., Messrs. J.   65
Cogswell and Harrison, Messrs.   17
Dougall and Sons, Messrs. J. D.   209
"Gye" Gun, The   155
Lancaster's Four-barrel Breech-loading Hammerless
    Pistol   23
Lancaster's Hammerless Lock for Wildfowl Guns ...   256
Reilly and Co., Messrs. C. M.   159
Tolley, Messrs. James W.   115

POEMS—

Fifty Years Ago. By Mowbray G. Malonek   272
First Meet, The. By Mowbray G. Malonek   175
Football. By H. C. Newton   228
For Winter again is Returning. By Mowbray G.
    Malonek   116
In the Shires. By H. C. Newton   158
Quiet to Ride and Drive. By Mowbray G. Malonek ...   200
St. Grouse. By H. C. Newton   24
St. Partridge. By H. C. Newton   66
St. Pheasant. By. H. C. Newton   114
Skating. By H. C. Newton   257
Trolling   261

REFLECTIONS—

Aquatics. By Diomed 46, 142
Athletics. By Diomed 43, 93, 143, 192, 240
Bicycling. By Diomed 94, 144, 191
Cricket. By Diomed 95, 140, 190
Dramatic. By Conn ...34, 86, 102, 180, 231, 276
Turfiana. By Tintagel 37
    ,, By Diomed 89, 135, 183, 234, 279

PARAGRAPHS—

Australian Batting Averages 18, 96, 104, 190
Eels Travelling over Land 275
Eclipse's First Race... 210
Hunting Cries 134
Old Days Fishing in the Thames 248
Some Large Pike 217
Sturgeon and Caviare 265

Volume Four

August 1882 - January 1883

Issue 19 : August 1882

Portrait of Robert Boyle (Earl of Cork)	(facing p1)
Biography - Robert Boyle [The Turf] by HBB	(p1-3)
Biography - Henry Ball [Athletics] by HBB	(p4-7)
Portrait of Henry Ball	(facing p4)
Biography - Jack Blackham [Cricket] by HBB	(p8-9)
Portrait of Alexander Bannerman	(facing p8)
Portrait of Jack Blackham	(facing p8)
Biography - Alexander Bannerman [Cricket] by HBB	(p10)
Portrait of Thomas Garrett	(facing p11)
Portrait of Thomas Horan	(facing p11)
Biography - Thomas Garrett [Cricket] by HBB	(p11)
Biography - Thomas Horan [Cricket] by HBB	(p12)
Lacrosse by Edwin Sachs	(p13-16)
Coaching: London to St.Albans	(p16)
Lithograph of The Desideratum New Hammerless Gun	(facing p17)
Our Gunmakers - Cogswell & Harrison by HBB	(p17-18)
The Australian Batting Averages	(p18)
A Gossip on Bream Fishing by Joseph Wheeldon	(p19-22)
Coaching and Picnic Knife	(p22)
Lithograph of Four-Barrel Breech Loading Pistol	(facing p23)
Lancaster's Four-Barrel Breech Loading Pistol by HBB	(p23)
St.Grouse [verses] by Henry Newton	(p24)
How to Use a Gun by Arthur Lane	(p25-29)
A Deal and a Sell [Fiction] by Austin Moray	(p30-33)
Before the Fight and After the Fight: Illustrations	(p33)
Dramatic Reflections	(p34-36)
July Reflections :	
Turfiana	(p37-43)
Athletics	(p43-45)
Aquatics	(p46-48)

[Edwin Thomas Sachs (1850-1910) was a sportswriter who spent twenty years on the staff at *The Field*. He was considered to be the 'father' of lacrosse in Britain. He edited numerous sporting books as well as having had published *Hockey & Lacrosse*]

Thomas Garrett

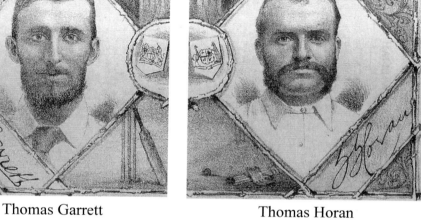

Thomas Horan

Cogswell & Harrison

Issue 20 - September 1882

Portrait of Ion Keith-Falconer (facing p49)
Biography - Ion Keith-Fletcher [Cycling] by HBB (p49-52)
Portrait of James Goater (facing p53)
Biography - James Goater [Jockey] by HBB (p53-55)
Biography - Charles Beal [Cricket] by HBB (p56)
Portrait of Charles Beal (facing p56)
The Pleasures of Racing by HBB (p57-59)
Biography - Harry Boyle [Cricket] by HBB (p60)
Portrait of Harry Boyle (facing p60)
Portrait of Percy McDonnell (facing p60)
Biography - Percy McDonnell [Cricket] by HBB (p61)
Equine Longevity by Martin Cobbett (p62-63)
Bailey's Patent Gas-Tight Cartridges by HBB (p64)
Lithograph of The Acme Hammerless Gun (facing p65)
Our Gunmakers - Beattie & Co by HBB (p65-66)
St.Partridge [verses] by Henry Newton (p66)
An Elopement Which Did Not Come Off by Arthur Lane (p67-73)
Old Pedestrian Jottings by HBB (p74-78)
Not Out: A Cricket Story [Fiction] by John Dawson (p79-82)
Book Review: *Lock to Lock* by Arthur Pask (p82)
Sailing on a Very Small Scale by Arthur Lane (p83-85)
Dramatic Reflections (p86-88)
Book Review: *The Scientific Angler* by David Foster (p88)
August Reflections :
        Turfiana (p89-92)
        Athletics (p93)
        Bicycling (p94)
        Cricket (p95-96)
The Australian Batting Averages (p96)

Issue 21 - October 1882

Portrait of Spencer Cavendish (Marquis of Hartington) (facing p97)
Biography - Spencer Cavendish [The Turf] by HBB (p97-100)
Portrait of Wallace Dudley-Ward (facing p101)
Biography - Wallace Dudley-Ward [Shooting] by HBB (p101)
Dramatic Reflections (p102-104)
The Australian Batting Averages (p104)
Beattie & Co.'s Community Hammerless Gun (p104)

Ion Keith-Falconer

James Goater

Charles Beal

Harry Boyle

Portrait of James Gibb (facing p105)
Biography - James Gibb [Athletics] by HBB (p105-107)
Biography - Hugh Massie [Cricket] by HBB (p108)
Portrait of George Palmer (facing p108)
Portrait of Hugh Massie (facing p108)
Biography - George Palmer [Cricket] by HBB (p109)
The Miseries of Racing by HBB (p110-114)
St.Pheasant [verses] by Henry Newton (p114)
Lithograph of The Perfection New Hammerless Gun (facing p115)
Our Gunmakers - Messrs Tolley by HBB (p115-116)
For Winter Again is Returning [verses] by Mowbray Malonek (p116)
A Very Queer Place by Joseph Wheeldon (p117-120)
Hunting Drawers - Hodgkinson (p120)
Gaur Shooting in India by William Scarth-Dixon (p121-129)
The Birmingham Sportsman's Exhibition by HBB (p130)
Cub-Hunting Memories by HBB (p131-134)
Hunting Cries: La Venerie de Jacques du Fouilloux (p134)
September Reflections :
    Turfiana (p135-139)
    Cricket (p140-141)
    Aquatics (p142)
    Athletics (p143)
    Bicycling (p144)

Issue 22 - November 1882

Portrait of John Russell (facing p145)
Biography - John Russell [Hunting] by Ernest Pearce (p145-148)
Portrait of John Roberts (facing p149)
Biography - John Roberts [Billiards] by HBB (p149-152)
Portrait of Herbert Sturt (facing p153)
Biography - Herbert Sturt [Athletics] by HBB (p153-154)
The Gye Gun by HBB (p155)
Biography - John Porter [The Turf] by HBB (p156-157)
Portrait of John Porter (facing p156)
In The Shires [verses] by Henry Newton (p158)
Lithograph of the Patent Hammerless Gun (facing p159)
Our Gunmakers - Reilly & Co. by HBB (p159-160)
A Clergyman (p160)
A Bit of Dubious Fishing by Joseph Wheeldon (p161-163)
A Chat About the Chifneys by William Lamonby (p164-168)

Percy McDonnell

Spencer Cavendish

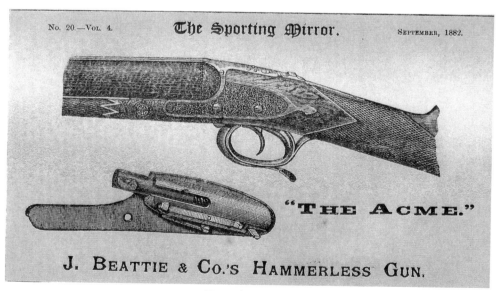

Beattie & Co

Pike Fishing in Winter by Wilfrid Pocklington (p169-171)
The Robberies of Racing by HBB (p172-175)
The First Meet [verses] by Mowbray Malonek (p175)
The Story of a Hunt [Fiction] by Hal Lowther (p176-179)
Dramatic Reflections (p180-182)
October Reflections :
    Turfiana (p183-189)
    Cricket (p190)
    Bicycling (p191)
    Athletics (p192)

Issue 23 - December 1882

Portrait of Thomas Lennard (facing p193)
Biography - Thomas Lennard [The Turf] by HBB (p193-195)
The Sportsman's Exhibition by HBB (p196)
Portrait of Arthur Lane (facing p197)
Biography - Arthur Lane [Shooting] by HBB (p197-199)
Quiet to Ride and Drive [verses] by Mowbray Malonek (p200)
Portrait of Sidney Baker (facing p201)
Biography - Sidney Baker [Athletics] by HBB (p201-204)
Portrait of Joseph Bennett (facing p205)
Biography - Joseph Bennett [Billiards] by HBB (p205-208)
Lithograph of Dougall's New Improved Hammerless Gun (facing p209)
Our Gunmakers - Dougall & Sons by HBB (p209-210)
Eclipse's First Race, 1769 (p210)
A Day's Spinning for Pike by Joseph Wheeldon (p211-213)
The Hard Work of Racing by HBB (p214-217)
Some Large Pike (p217)
Fox Hunting and Fox Hunters by HBB (p218-220)
California Deer Hunt (p220)
Snipe Shooting in the Fens by Hal Forester (p221-223)
Horses' Feet and How to Treat Them by HBB (p224-225)
Jockeys' Mounts 1882 (p225)
With the Quorn at Kirby Gate by William Blew (p226-228)
Football [verses] by Henry Newton (p228)
Some Peculiar Matches by William Lamonby (p229-230)
Dramatic Reflections (p231-233)
November Reflections :
    Turfiana (p234-239)
    Athletics (p240)

Wallace Dudley-Ward

James Gibb

Hugh Massie

George Palmer

Issue 24 : January 1883

Portrait of George Harris [Lord Harris]   (facing p241)
Biography - George Harris [Cricket] by HBB   (p241-244)
Portrait of Henry Savile   (facing p245)
Biography - Henry Savile [The Turf] by HBB   (p245-248)
Old Days' Fishing on the Thames by Edward Jesse   (p248)
Portrait of Francis Wood   (facing p249)
Biography - Francis Wood [Athletics] by HBB   (p249-252)
Portrait of William Peall   (facing p253)
Biography - William Peall [Billiards] by HBB   (p253-255)
Our Gunmakers - Charles Lancaster by HBB   (p256-257)
Lithograph of Lancaster's Lock for Wildfowl Guns   (facing p256)
Skating [verses] by Henry Newton   (p257)
Skating in the Fens by Hal Forester   (p258-261)
The Sportsman's Exhibition by HBB   (p261)
Rod and Trigger - A Mixed Bag by HBB   (p262-265)
Sturgeon and Caviare [on the Delaware River]   (p265)
The Cottesmore Hunt by William Blew   (p266-267)
The Integrity of Racing by HBB   (p268-271)
Trolling [verses] by William Watts   (p271)
Fifty Years Ago [verses] by Mowbray Malonek   (p272)
American Courtesy by Martin Cobbett   (p273-275)
Eels Travelling Over Land by Edward Jesse   (p275)
Dramatic Reflections   (p276-278)
December Reflections : Turfiana   (p279-284)

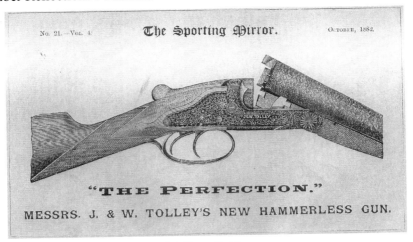

Tolley & Co

John Russell

John Roberts

Herbert Sturt

John Porter

Thomas Lennard

ONE WHO HAS FIRED SOME
20,000 TRIAL SHOTS AT MARKS.

Arthur Lane

Sidney Baker

Joseph Bennett

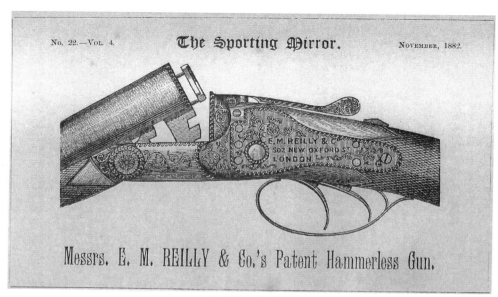

Reilly & Co

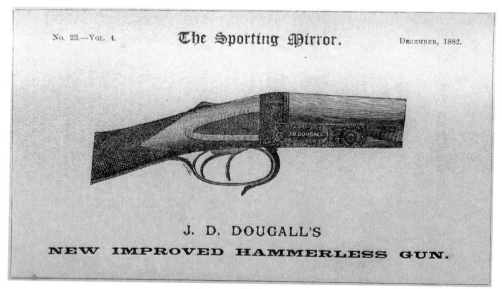

Dougall & Sons

George Harris

THE LATE
MENRY SAVILE.

Henry Savile

Francis Wood

William Peall

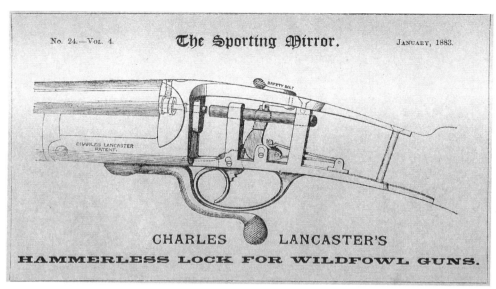

Lancaster & Co

Lancaster - pistol

THE SPORTING MIRROR

EDITED BY
"DIOMED".

CELEBRITIES, VOTARIES, PORTRAITS,
BIOGRAPHIES, DOINGS.

Volume V.

JANUARY TO JUNE.

1883

HARRY ETHERINGTON, 152, Fleet Street, London, E.C.

Greener's Gun

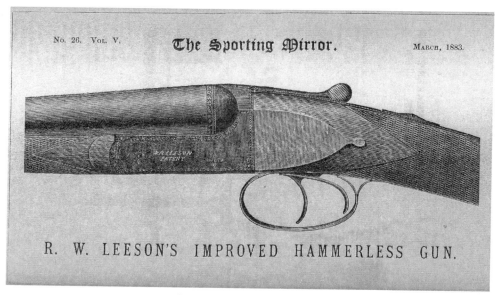

Leeson's Hammerless

INDEX.

ARTICLES—

                                                               PAGE

	PAGE
A Day with the Pike. By H. B. Bromhead	271
At Hyde Park, Sheffield. By Hal Lowther	127
Athletic Prospects. By G. P. B....	235
Badger Hunting. By Wilf. Pocklington	143
Belvoir Hunt, The. By Old Towler	24
Bit of Rabbiting, A. By Wilf. Pocklington	238
Carp, and Carp Fishing. By Cyprinus ...	228
Chat about Eclipse, A. By Hal Forester	136
Chance Fishing in Lakes and Ponds. By J. P. Wheeldon	79
Coaching, and the Wonder Coach. By Helvellyn	232
Day with the Pike, A. By H. B. Bromhead	
Day's Rabbit Shooting, A. By Hal Forester	21
Death and Turf Nominations. By Diomed	130
Deer Hunting in Colorado. By S. L.	244
Fish Ladders. By A. A. ...	283
Fishing in Ireland. By Wilf. Pocklington	86
From Murky Fog to Golden Sunshine. By J. P. Wheeldon	31
George IV. and the Turf. By Helvellyn	286
In the North Sea. By Wildfowler	84
New "Perfect" Shells, The. By One who has Fired 20,000 Trial Shots at Marks ...	27
Otter Hunting in Ireland. By Cherry Brandy	279
Our Turf Talent. By Argus Eye	188
Our Opening Day. By H. B. Bromhead	146
Paternostering for Pike. By J. P. Wheeldon ...	133
Passing the Proof. By Alfred Allison ...	173
Past and Present. By H. B. Bromhead	180
Pike Fishing and Pike Fishers. By H. B. Bromhead...	34
Poachers' Paraphernalia. By Alfred Allison	224
Racing, The Game of. By H. B. Bromhead	17
Reminiscences of Tom Sayers. In three chapters. By W. A.	89, 139, 183
Some Old Turf Chat. By Helvellyn	193
Some Early American Racing. By H. B. Bromhead ...	73
Some Winter Sport. By Wilf. Pocklington	
Sportsman's Exhibition, The. By Diomed	49, 101
Winter Hunting in Montana. By Wilf. Pocklington ...	190
Wonderful Cricketing Feats. By Hal Forester	177
Word about Rooks, A. By Hal Forester	242

BIOGRAPHIES AND PORTRAITS—

	PAGE
Austria, The Emperor of ...	1
Batthyany, The late Prince of	209
Beckley, George Philip	216
Chambers, The late John Graham	121
Coupland, John	163
Crawfurd, The late W. Stirling	116
Fox, George Lane ...	61
Galway, Lord	161
Guillemard, A. G. ...	166
Hamilton, The Duke of	57
Kemp, M. C....	260
Middleton, Captain W. G. ...	13
Mitchell, William ...	65

BIOGRAPHIES AND PORTRAITS (*Continued*)—   PAGE

Montrose, The Duke of 214
Petrie, A. Gordon 63
Portsmouth, The Earl of 113
Renshaw, W. 263
Rutland, The Duke of 4
Shrewsbury, Arthur 265
Stamford and Warrington, The late Earl of 8
Stanley, Sackville West 169
Topping, Robert 124
Yarborough, The Earl of 257
"Young Nimrod," Charles Brown 220

OUR GUNMAKERS—

Bland's Extracting Army Revolver 171
Gibbs, George 269
Greener, W. W. 14
Lancaster's New Machine for Closing Kynoch's
   "Perfect" Cases ... ...
Leeson, W. W. 69
Turner, Thomas 222

PARAGRAPHS—

Angling as a Medicine 135
Captain Ross in 1835 227
Dolphin in Mythology, The 94
Fragrant Weed, The 132
Happy Life of an Angler, The 88
Salmon Fishing on the Columbia River 231
Sport Extraordinary 240
Superstitions concerning Fish 88
Tickling Trout 148
Vitality of the Trout 129

POEMS—

October in Colorado. By S. L. 275
April Arrangements. By H. C. Newton 160
At the Squire's. By M. G. Malonek 149
February Fixtures. By H. C. Newton 20
For Summer, Bright Summer's Returning. By M. G.
   Malonek 176
How Old Basher Caught Salmon 37
Jingle on July, A. By H. C. Newton 289
June Jottings. By H. C. Newton 241
March Memoranda. By H. C. Newton 83
May Meetings. By H. C. Newton 170
Rare Bit of Stuff, A. By M. G. Malonek 72
Veteran's Farewell, The. By M. G. Malonek 78

REFLECTIONS—

Aquatics. By Diomed 48, 159, 208
Athletics. By Diomed 207
Coursing 100
Cricket. By Diomed 45, 206
Dramatic. By Conn 38, 95, 150, 196, 246, 290
Football. By Diomed 46
Pigeon Shooting. By Diomed 158
Turñana. By Diomed 41, 98, 153, 199, 249, 293

Volume Five

February - July 1883

Issue 25 : February 1883

Portrait of Elisabeth Joseph (Empress of Austria)	(facing p1)
Biography - Elisabeth Joseph [Hunting] by HBB	(p1-3)
Biography - Charles Manners [The Turf] by HBB	(p4-7)
Portrait of Charles Manners (Duke of Rutland)	(facing p4)
Biography - George Grey [The Turf] by HBB	(p8-12)
Portrait of George Grey (Earl of Stamford)	(facing p8)
Portrait of George Middleton by HBB	(facing p13)
Biography - George Middleton [The Turf] by HBB	(p13)
Our Gunmakers - Greener's (with diagrams) by HBB	(p14-16)
Lithograph of Greener's Ejecting Hammerless Gun	(facing p14)
Weather Wisdom [verses]	(p16)
The Game of Racing by HBB	(p17-20)
February Fixtures [verses] by Henry Newton	(p20)
A Day's Rabbit Shooting by Hal Forester	(p21-23)
Two-Eyed Sight	(p23)
The Belvoir Hunt by William Blew	(p24-26)
A Well-Fitting Hat	(p26)
The New Perfect Shells by Arthur Lane	(p27-30)
From Murky Fog to Golden Sunshine by Joseph Wheeldon	(p31-33)
Pike Fishing and Pike Fishers by HBB	(p34-37)
How Old Barker Caught Salmon [verses]	(p37)
Dramatic Reflections	(p38-40)
January Reflections :	
Turfiana	(p41-44)
Cricket	(p45)
Football [Association/Rugby]	(p46-47)
Aquatics	(p48)
The Sportsman's Exhibition by HBB	(p49-56)

Issue 26 : March 1883

Portrait of William Douglas-Hamilton (Duke of Hamilton)	(facing p57)
Biography - William Douglas-Hamilton [The Turf] by HBB	(p57-60)
Portrait of George Lane-Fox	(facing p61)
Biography - George Lane-Fox [Hunting] by HBB	(p61-62)

Elisabeth Joseph

Charles Manners

George Grey

George Middleton

Portrait of Gordon Petrie	(facing p63)
Biography - Gordon Petrie [Rugby Union] by HBB	(p63-64)
Portrait of William Mitchell	(facing p65)
Biography - William Mitchell [Billiards] by HBB	(p65-68)
Lithograph of Leeson's Hammerless Gun	(facing p69)
Our Gunmakers - Leeson's (with diagrams) by HBB	(p69-70)
Charles Lancaster's Closing Kynoch (with diagram) by HBB	(p71-72)
A Rare Bit of Stuff [verses] by Mowbray Malonek	(p72)
Some Early American Racing by HBB	(p73-77)
The Veteran's Farewell [verses] by Mowbray Malonek	(p78)
Chance Fishing in Lakes and Ponds by Joseph Wheeldon	(p79-82)
War Department - Specification of Powder	(p82)
March Memoranda [verses] by Henry Newton	(p83)
In the North Sea by Lewis Clements	(p84-85)
Fishing in Ireland by Wilfrid Pocklington	(p86-88)
The Happy Life of an Angler	(p88)
Superstitions Concerning Fish	(p88)
Reminiscences of Tom Sayers (Part One) by Waller Ashe	(p89-94)
The Dolphin in Mythology	(p94)
Dramatic Reflections	(p95-97)
February Reflections :	
Turfiana	(p98-100)
Coursing	(p100)
The Sportsman's Exhibition by HBB	(p101-112)

[Lewis Clements contributed to a number of magazines including *Bell's Life; Sporting Gazette* and *The Field* before becoming editor of *Shooting Times*. He wrote a number of books such as *Shooting & Fishing Trips; Modern Wildfowling* and *Shooting Adventures*]

Issue 27 : April 1883

Portrait of Isaac Fellowes (Earl of Portsmouth)	(facing p113)
Biography - Isaac Fellowes [The Turf] by HBB	(p113-115)
Biography - Stirling Crawfurd [The Turf] by HBB	(p116-120)
Portrait of Stirling Crawfurd	(facing p116)
Portrait of John Chambers	(facing p121)
Biography - John Chambers [Sporting Journalist] by HBB	(p121-123)
Biography - Robert Topping [Bookmaker] by HBB	(p124-126)
Portrait of Robert Topping	(facing p124)
At Hyde Park, Sheffield by Hal Lowther	(p127-129)

William Douglas-Hamilton

George Lane-Fox

Gordon Petrie

William Mitchell

Vitality of the Trout (p129)
Death and Turf Nominations by HBB (p130-132)
The Fragrant Weed by Peyton Ward (p132)
Paternostering for Pike by Joseph Wheeldon (p133-135)
Angling as a Medicine by George Dawson (p135)
A Chat About Eclipse by Hal Forester (p136-138)
Reminiscences of Tom Sayers (Part Two) by Waller Ashe (p139-142)
Badger Hunting by Wilfrid Pocklington (p143-145)
Our Opening Day by HBB (p146-148)
Tickling Trout (p148)
At the Squires [verses] by Wilfrid Pocklington (p149)
Dramatic Reflections (p150-152)
March Reflections :
      Turfiana (p153-157)
      Pigeon Shooting (p158)
      Aquatics (p159)
April Arrangements [verses] by Henry Newton (p160)

Issue 28 : May 1883

Portrait of George Monckton-Arundell (Lord Galway) (facing p161)
Biography - George Monckton-Arundell [The Turf] by HBB (p162-162)
Portrait of John Coupland (facing p163)
Biography - John Coupland [Hunting] by HBB (p163-165)
Lancaster Rifles by Frank Morrison (p165)
Biography - Arthur Guillemard [Rugby Union] by HBB (p166-168)
Portrait of Arthur Guillemard (facing p166)
Portrait of Sackville Stanley (facing p169)
Biography - Sackville Stanley [Billiards] by HBB (p169)
May Meetings [verses] by Henry Newton (p170)
Lithograph of Bland's Self Extracting Army Revolver (facing p171)
Our Gunmakers - Bland & Sons (with diagrams) by HBB (p171-172)
British Kennel Association Dog Show (p172)
Passing the Proof by Alfred Allison (p173-175)
For Summer, Bright Summer's Returning [verses] by Mowbray Malonek (p176)
Wonderful Cricketing Feats by Hal Forester (p177-179)
Past and Present by HBB (p180-182)
Reminiscences of Tom Sayers (Part Three) by Waller Ashe (p183-187)
Our Turf Talent by Martin Cobbett (p188-189)
Winter Hunting in Montana by Wilfrid Pocklington (p190-192)
Sporting Novelties (p192)

Isaac Fellowes

Stirling Crawfurd

John Chambers

Robert Topping

Some Old Turf Chat by William Lamonby (p193-195)
Dramatic Reflections (p196-198)
April Reflections :
      Turfiana (p199-205)
      Cricket (p206)
      Athletics (p207)
      Aquatics (p208)

[Alfred Allison was editor of *The Sportsman*. He contributed to *Bell's Life* and to numerous other magazines]

Issue 29 : June 1883

Portrait of Gustavus Batthyany (facing p209)
Biography - Gustavus Batthyany [The Turf] by HBB (p209-213)
Biography - Douglas Graham [The Turf] by HBB (p214-215)
Portrait of Douglas Graham (Duke of Montrose) (facing p214)
Transvaal: The South African Syndicate Company (p215)
Biography - George Beckley [Athletics] by HBB (p216-219)
Portrait of George Beckley (facing p216)
Biography - Charles Brown [Shooting] by HBB (p220-221)
Portrait of Charles Brown (facing p220)
Our Gunmakers - Thomas Turner by HBB (p222-223)
Lithograph of Turner's Featherweight Gun (facing p222)
Lines [verses] by Mowbray Malonek (p223)
Turnbull & Wood's Old Highland Whisky (p223)
Poachers Paraphernalia by Alfred Allison (p224-227)
Captain Horatio Ross in 1835 (p227)
Carp and Carp Fishing by Alfred Allison (p228-231)
Lawn Tennis - Prosser's Racquets and Balls (p231)
Salmon Fishing on the Columbia River (p231)
Coaching and the Wonder Coach by William Lamonby (p232-234)
Ellis's Patent Boot Studs (p234)
Athletic Prospects by George Beckley (p235-237)
Mitrailleuse Mineral Oil Burner (p237)
A Bit of Rabbiting by Wilfrid Pocklington (p238-240)
Wildfowling: Hunt on Lake Fezzara (p240)
June Jottings [verses] by Henry Newton (p241)
A Word About Rooks by Hal Forester (p242-243)
Deer Hunting in Colorado by Stewart Laird (p244-245)
Dramatic Reflections (p246-248)
May Reflections : Turfiana (p249-256)

George Monckton-Arundell

John Coupland

Arthur Guillemard

Sackville Stanley

Issue 30 : July 1883

Portrait of Charles Pelham (Earl of Yarborough)	(facing p257)
Biography - Charles Pelham [Hunting] by HBB	(p257-259)
Biography - Manley Kemp [Cricket] by HBB	(p260-262)
Portrait of Manley Kemp	(facing p260)
Portrait of William Renshaw	(facing p263)
Biography - William Renshaw [Lawn Tennis] by HBB	(p263-264)
Portrait of Arthur Shrewsbury	(facing p265)
Biography - Arthur Shrewsbury [Cricket] by HBB	(p265-268)
Lithograph of Gibb's Top Lever Hammerless Gun	(facing p269)
Our Gunmakers - George Gibbs by HBB	(p269-270)
A Day With the Pike by HBB	(p271-275)
October in Colorado [verses] by Stewart Laird	(p275)
New Safety Saddle Bar	(p275)
Some Winter Sport by Wilfrid Pocklington	(p276-278)
The Waterloo Lawn Tennis Bat	(p278)
Otter Hunting in Ireland by George Lowth	(p279-282)
Fish Ladders by Alfred Allinson	(p283-285)
George IV and the Turf by William Lamonby	(p286-288)
Boyden's Medals	(p288)
Pitt's Mineral and Aerated Waters	(p288)
Maitland's St.Andrew's Whisky	(p288)
Cary's Binoculars	(p288)
A Jingle on July [verses] by Henry Newton	(p289)
Dramatic Reflections	(p290-292)
June Reflections : Turfiana	(p293-300)

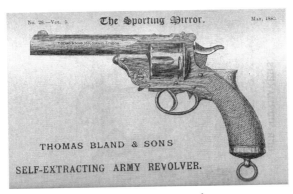

Bland's Army Revolver

Gustavus Batthyany

Douglas Graham

George Beckley

Charles Brown

Charles Pelham

Manley Kemp

William Renshaw

Arthur Shrewsbury

Turner's Featherweight

Gibbs' Hammerless

THE SPORTING MIRROR

CELEBRITIES, VOTARIES, PORTRAITS, BIOGRAPHIES, DOINGS.

Volume VI.

JULY TO DECEMBER.

1883.

HARRY ETHERINGTON, 152, Fleet Street, London, E.C.

Lancaster's Rifle

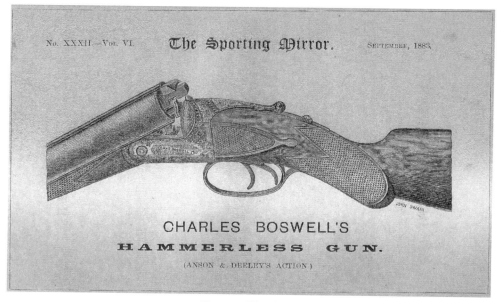

Boswell's Gun

INDEX.

ARTICLES—   PAGE

Audi Alteram Partem. By Borderer...   261
An Authority Hoist with his Own Petard. By A. J. Uggins   ...   235
A Voice from the Bush. By Dum Spiro Spero   80
An Important Arrival. By Waverley   109
An Explosive Experience in the Netherlands. By Camico   ...   172
A Run in the Open. By H.V.L.S.   224
Black Tuesday. By Waverley...   158
Brand New. By A. Allison   119
Besieged in Ireland. By Austin Moray   37
Cricket in 1883. By J.B.T.   116
Experiences at a Boar Hunt. By Wilf. Pocklington   29
Football at the Fall of the Leaf. By H.V.L.S.   166
Football Facts and Frolics. By International   215
Grouse and the Grisly Terror. By an Old Army Surgeon   ...   75
Great Fairfield Meeting, The   256
Horses and Horse Racing of the Past. By H.L.   44
Horsey Yarn, A. By A.T.S. 77, 141, 169, 221 284
Leaves from my American Diary. By Wissahickon   ...   162, 253
My Double Catch at Margate. By the Happy One   ...   175, 271
Middle Park. By John Mitchell   125
Masters of Hunts. By Helvellyn   22
Miller and His Merry Men. By A. Allison...   62
My First Rat Hunt. By Waverley   68
More from the Bush. By Dum Spiro Spero   218
Patrons of the Punch Bowl. By Waverley...   210
Pleasures of Fishing, The. By H. B. Bromhead   26
Recollections of Jerome Park. By Annie Wakeman   70
Settling the Hunt Succession. By Plantagenet   206
Some South Coast Rowers. By Martin Cobbett   128
Some Steeplechasing Chat. By F. Morrison   33
Sports Renaissance. By The Seer   64
Sealing in the North Sea. By Camico   87
Tufting for Red Deer. By Plantagenet   112
Winter's Pastime, A. By J. B. T.   180
Yachting Notes. By. C. J. Craig   42

BIOGRAPHIES AND PORTRAITS—

Bisset, Mordaunt Fenwick, M.P.   145
Craven, The Earl of   241
Coleman, G. Pembroke   250
Drogheda, Marquis of   193
Falmouth, Lord   1
Gaskell, H. W.   12
Gulston, F. S.   148
Innes, W. J.   247
Hawke, The Hon. M. Bladen   8
Lonsdale, The Earl of   49
Lucas, A. Perry   56
Liles, C. E.   152
Labat, R. H.   200
March, Earl of   97
Machell, Captain...   191
Peck, Robert   102
Reynolds, H. R., Jun.   54
Sadler, J. D.   155

95

BIOGRAPHIES AND PORTRAITS (*Continued*)—   PAGE

Snook, William   15
Studd, C. T.   106
Trelawney, The Late Charles   99
Webb, Captain Matthew   51
Wood, F.   203

POEMS—

August Anticipations.   By H. C. Newton   32
Arcades Ambo.   By J. Maycock   139
An Ancient War Horse.   By Ninas   179
An Astronomical Rhapsodie.   By J. Maycock   223
Crumpled Rose Leaf, The.   By Camico   20
Camp Fire, The.   By Nimrod   36
Cruel Kindness.   By J. Maycock   59
Good Resolutions.   By J. Maycock   165
How we Beat the Favourite   122
Hunting Lay, A.   By H. C. Newton   260
New Year's Notes   280
Sporting Interrogatory.   By our Hanwell Hunter   74
The Angling Ananias   213

MISCELLANEOUS—

A Hat Case Full of Money   28
A Tale of The Church   31
A Ducal Editor   144
Auriferous Aquatics   144
Another New Racecourse   214
Canoeing—The Tame and Trent   274
Cross-country Runners   271
Blow for Backers, A   42
Bicycle Accidents in the City   101
Catching a Bear with Salt   21
Calcutta International Exhibition   61
Close of the Summer Coaching Season   144
Champion Canine Swimmer, A   239
Dramatic Reflections.   By Conn   46
Death of W. Gilbert   55
Ducks Migrating   239
English and Canadian Cricket   202
Faithful Dog, A...   226
Internationalisation of Sport   73
Hanlan and Courtney   60
He Drew a Blank   161
Mapping out the Cricket Campaign   281
Novel Velocipede Race   76
Notes Dramatic and Musical.   By Annotator ... 93, 135, 189, 237, 286
Opening of the Coursing Season   124
Our Book Case.   By Old Dryasdust 192, 240, 288
Puritans in the Colonies   178
Ravens as Carriers   234
Run by Moonlight, A   236
Sportsmen Increasing in England   101
Snipe Tale, A   151
Southern Huntress Takes the Veil, A   240
Turf Siftings.   By Greensward 83, 130, 183, 227, 266
There were Wonders in those Days   191
Thames Leaving Teddington   202
To see Ourselves as Others see Us   213
Unusual Sport   188
Whitehaired Trout, A   188
Yachting Gossip.   By Hold to Windward   90
Yorkshire Stirring   138

Volume Six

August 1883 - January 1884

Issue 31 : August 1883

Portrait of Evelyn Boscawen (Lord Falmouth)	(facing p1)
Biography - Evelyn Boscawen [The Turf] by HBB	(p1-7)
Biography - Martin Hawke [Cricket] by HBB	(p8-11)
Portrait of Martin Hawke (Lord Hawke)	(facing p8)
Biography - Herbert Gaskell [Cycling] by HBB	(p12-14)
Portrait of Herbert Gaskell	(facing p12)
The Power of a Crocodile's Jaw	(p14)
Portrait of William Snook	(facing p15)
Biography - William Snook [Athletics] by HBB	(p15-19)
Our Gunmakers - Charles Lancaster by HBB	(p20)
Lithograph of Lancaster's Miniature Match Rifle	(facing p20)
Thomas Turner's Attachable Muzzle (with diagrams) by HBB	(p21)
Catching a Bear With Salt	(p21)
Master of Hounds by William Lamonby	(p22-25)
Pot-8-os [Horse]	(p25)
The Pleasures of Fishing by HBB	(p26-28)
A Hat Case Full of Money by James Rice	(p28)
Experiences at a Boar Hunt by Wilfrid Pocklington	(p29-31)
A Diver Attacked by a Pike	(p31)
A Tale of the Church	(p31)
August Anticipations [verses] by Henry Newton	(p32)
Some Steeplechasing Chat by Frank Morrison	(p33-36)
The Camp Fire [verses] by Thomas Gordon	(p36)
Besieged in Ireland by Austin Moray	(p37-41)
Yachting Notes by Charles Craig	(p42-43)
Horses and Horse Racing of the Past by Harold Leeney	(p44-45)
Dramatic Reflections	(p46-48)

Issue 32 : September 1883

Portrait of Hugh Lowther (Earl of Lonsdale)	(facing p49)
Biography - Hugh Lowther [Hunting/The Turf] by HBB	(p49-50)
Pigeon Shooting Bill	(p50)
Portrait of Matthew Webb	(facing p51)
Biography - Matthew Webb [Swimming] by HBB	(p51-53)

Evelyn Boscawen

Martin Hawke

Herbert Gaskell

William Snook

Biography - Harry Reynolds [Cycling] by HBB	(p54-55)
Portrait of Harry Reynolds	(facing p54)
Death of William Gilbert	(p55)
Biography - Alfred Lucas [Cricket] by HBB	(p56-58)
Portrait of Alfred Lucas	(facing p56)
Cruel Kindness [verses] by James Maycock	(p59)
Our Gunmakers - Charles Boswell by HBB	(p60)
Lithograph of Boswell's Hammerless Gun	(facing p60)
Calcutta International Exhibition	(p61)
Hanlan and Courtney [Chantanqua Lake Race]	(p61)
Miller and his Merry Men (Piscatorial) by Alfred Allison	(p62-63)
Sports Renaissance - Picture of Twentieth Century England	(p64-67)
My First Rat Hunt	(p68-69)
After the Exhibition is Over	(p69)
Recollections of Jerome Park by Annie Wakeman	(p70-73)
Fishermen's Congress	(p73)
Internationalisation of Sport: Victoria Trotting Club	(p73)
A Sporting Interrogatory [verses]	(p74)
Grouse and the Grisly Terror	(p75-76)
A Novel Velocipede Race (Sunday Newspaper Deliveries)	(p76)
A Horsey Yarn (part one)	(p77-79)
Water-Proofing Material	(p79)
A Voice From the Bush (cricket)	(p80-82)
Liquid Insect Exterminator	(p82)
A Blow for Backers (Lord Falmouth's Horses)	(p82)
Turf Siftings by William Lamonby	(p83-86)
Sealing in the North Sea	(p87-89)
Yachting Gossip by Dixon Kemp	(p90-92)
Lamplough's Pyretic Saline	(p92)
Prolongation of the Fisheries Exhibition	(p92)
Notes Dramatic and Musical	(p93-96)
Grouse Shooting Season	(p96)

Issue 33 : October 1883

Portrait of Charles Lennox (Earl of March)	(facing p97)
Biography - Charles Lennox [The Turf] by HBB	(p97-98)
Portrait of Charles Trelawny	(facing p99)
Biography - Charles Trelawny [Hunting] by Ernest Pearce	(p99-101)
Sportsmen Increasing in England (Gun & Game Licences)	(p101)
Bicycle Accidents in the City (of London)	(p101)

Hugh Lowther

Matthew Webb

Harry Reynolds

Alfred Lucas

Biography - Robert Peck [The Turf] by HBB	(p102-105)
Portrait of Robert Peck	(facing p102)
Biography - Charles Studd [Cricket] by HBB	(p106-108)
Portrait of Charles Studd	(facing p106)
An Important Arrival [Fiction]	(p109-111)
Tufting for Red Deer by Ernest Pearce	(p112-115)
International Congress of Ornithologists	(p115)
Cricket in 1883 by John Thomson	(p116-118)
Piscatorial Pictures by Alfred Allison	(p119-121)
How We Beat the Favourite [verses]	(p122-124)
Robert Bateson-Harvey's Harriers	(p124)
Opening of the Coursing Season	(p124)
Middle Park [Eltham] by HBB	(p125-127)
Poultry Shows	(p127)
Some South Coast Rowers by Martin Cobbett	(p128-129)
Turf Siftings by William Lamonby	(p130-134)
Notes Dramatic and Musical	(p135-138)
Her Majesty's Staghounds	(p138)
Yorkshire Stirring - Proposed Racecourse at Heddon	(p138)
Westaway's Patent Guidance Carriage Lamps	(p138)
Arcades Ambo [verses] by James Maycock	(p139)
Diana Gunpowder by HBB	(p140)
Newmarket Horse Clippers	(p140)
A Horsey Yarn (part two)	(p141-144)
Autumnal Coaching - The Old Times coach	(p144)
A Ducal Editor [The Badminton Series of Sporting Books]	(p144)
Auriferous Aquatics [Edward Hanlan's Winnings]	(p144)
Close of the Summer Coaching Season	(p144)
The Patent Collapsible Postal Parcel Bag	(p144)

[Ernest Pearce spent the early part of his career working at *The Field*, rising to be one of the hunting correspondents. He then became a distinguished war reporter, especially during the Boer War]

Issue 34 : November 1883

Portrait of Mordaunt Fenwick-Bisset	(facing p145)
Biography - Mordaunt Fenwick-Bisset [Hunting] by Ernest Pearce	(p145-147)
Biography - Francis (Frank) Gulston [Rowing] by HBB	(p148-151)
Portrait of Francis (Frank) Gulston	(facing p148)
A Snipe Tale	(p151)

Charles Lennox

Charles Trelawny

Robert Peck

Charles Studd

Biography - Charles Liles [Cycling] by HBB (p152-154)
Portrait of Charles Liles (facing p152)
Portrait of James Sadler (facing p155)
Biography - James Sadler [Athletics] by HBB (p155-157)
Black Tuesday - A Coursing Sketch [Fiction] (p158-161)
He Drew a Blank [Metropolitan Swimming Club Member] (p161)
Leaves From My American Diary - The Susquehanna River (part one) (p162-164)
America's Business City Advances - Chicago [Jockey] Club (p164)
Good Resolutions [verses] by James Maycock (p165)
Football at the Fall of the Leaf [Association/Rugby] by Henry Stanton (p166-168)
A Horsey Yarn (part three) (p169-171)
An Explosive Experience in the Netherlands (p172-174)
My Double Catch at Margate (part one) [Fiction] (p175-178)
The Puritans in the Colonies - South Australia (p178)
Calf versus Horse [Race] (p178)
An Ancient War Horse [verses] (p179)
A Winter's Pastime [Billiards] by John Thomson (p180-182)
Turf Siftings by William Lamonby (p183-188)
A White Haired Trout (p188)
Unusual Sport [Fishing] (p188)
Notes Dramatic and Musical (p189-191)
There Were Wonders in Those Days [Sheaf Binding] (p191)
Our Bookcase :
    Scratch Team of Essays by Septimus Berdmore (p192)
    Indian Racing Reminiscences by Horace Hayes (p192)
    The Patents, Designs & Trade Marks Act by James Johnson (p192)

[Henry Valentine Labron Stanton (1859-1933) originally trained as a solicitor but soon moved into sporting journalism. He spent most of his career on the staff of *The Sportsman*. He wrote the *Cricketers' and Footballers' Birthday Book* as well as *The Rise of Rugby Football*. He did much for *Wisden's Almanack*]

Issue 35 : December 1883

Portrait of Henry Moore (Marquis of Drogheda) (facing p193)
Biography - Henry Moore [The Turf] by HBB (p193-195)
Biography - James Machell [The Turf] by HBB (p196-199)
Portrait of James Machell (facing p196)
Biography - Robert Labat [Rowing] by HBB (p200-202)
Portrait of Robert Labat (facing p200)
English and Canadian Cricket (p202)

Mordaunt Fenwick-Bisset

Frank Gulston

Charles Liles

James Sadler

The Thames Leaving Teddington [Proposed Lock]   (p202)
Portrait of Frederick Wood   (facing p203)
Biography - Frederick Wood [Cycling] by HBB   (p203-205)
Settling the Hunt Succession by Ernest Pearce   (p206-208)
The Crumpled Rose Leaf [verses]   (p209)
Patrons of the Punch Bowl   (p210-213)
To See Ourselves as Others See Us   (p213)
The Angling Ananias [verses]   (p213)
Another New Racecourse [Kingston-upon-Hull]   (p214)
Football Facts and Frolics [Association/Rugby] by Henry Stanton (p215-217)
Australian Sporting Papers   (p217)
More From the Bush   (p218-220)
A Horsey Yarn (part four)   (p221-222)
An Astronomical Rhapsodie [verses] by James Maycock   (p223)
A Run in the Open [Cross-Country] by Henry Stanton   (p224-226)
Bicycling [Boston Bicycle Club]   (p226)
A Faithful Dog   (p226)
Turf Siftings by William Lamonby   (p227-231)
Horse Show at New York   (p231)
Turned to Clay (with Diagrams)   (p232-234)
Ravens as Carriers   (p234)
An Authority Hoist With His Own Petard   (p235-236)
A Run by Moonlight [From the *Campbell County Record*]   (p236)
Notes Dramatic and Musical   (p237-239)
Ducks Migrating   (p239)
A Champion Canine Swimmer   (p239)
Our Bookcase : [All Musical]
        The Harmonium Cabinet by Robert Pitman   (p240)
        Forest Echoes by William Lancelot   (p240)
        The Cameron by Herbert Godfrey   (p240)
        Musical Monthly [Issues One and Two]   (p240)
        The Fellow That Looks Like Me by Harry Leslie   (p240)
A Southern Huntress Takes the Veil [Elkridge Hunt Club]   (p240)

Issue 36 : January 1884

Portrait of George Craven (Earl of Craven)   (facing p241)
Biography - George Craven [Coursing] by HBB   (p241-243)
Young Ringfence   (p243)
Coloured Feathers in Game   (p243)
Biography - Garrett Moore [Jockey] by HBB   (p244-246)

Henry Moore

James Machell

Robert Labat

Frederick Wood

Portrait of Garrett Moore	(facing p244)
Prince Kung [Chinese Artificial Garden]	(p246)
Portrait of William Innes	(facing p247)
Biography - William Innes [Sporting Journalist] by HBB	(p247-249)
Making Game of the Dude	(p249)
A Flash of Lightning [Russian Stables]	(p249)
Biography - Pembroke Coleman [Cycling] by HBB	(p250-252)
Portrait of Pembroke Coleman	(facing p250)
Leaves From my American Diary - The Susquehanna River (part two)	(p253-255)
A Melbourne Owner	(p255)
The Great Fairfield Meeting [Fiction]	(p256-259)
Slaughter of Buffalo	(p259)
A Hunting Lay [verses] by Henry Newton	(p260)
Audi Alteram Partem by Richard Green-Price	(p261-265)
Narrow Heels in Horses	(p265)
Death of Stonewall Jackson [Kenton County Club]	(p265)
Turf Siftings by William Lamonby	(p266-270)
Tattersall's Cup at Randwick	(p270)
My Double Catch at Margate (part two) [Fiction]	(p271-274)
A Northumbrian Lady	(p274)
Cross-Country Runners	(p274)
Canoeing by Edward Humphreys	(p275-279)
New Year's Notes [verses] by Henry Newton	(p280)
Mapping Out the Cricket Campaign (for 1884) by Henry Stanton	(p281-283)
Vertical and Horizontal Steam Engines	(p283)
A Horsey Yarn (part five)	(p284-285)
Notes Dramatic and Musical	(p286-287)
Our Bookcase :	
Our Friend the Dog by Gordon Stables	(p288)
Australian Cricketer's Guide by Harry Boyle & David Scott	(p288)
Highland Sportsman by Robert Hall	(p288)
Wildfowler's Dog Breaking by Lewis Clements	(p288)
Book-keeping Simplified by Henry Feast	(p288)

[Richard Green-Price (1838-1909) was a contributor to many sporting magazines and an author of numerous books. He was always keen about hounds and hunting particularly in his home county of Radnorshire and neighbouring Shropshire. His main periodicals were *The Field* and *Baily's Magazine of Sports and Pastimes*]

George Craven

Garrett Moore

William Innes

Pembroke Coleman

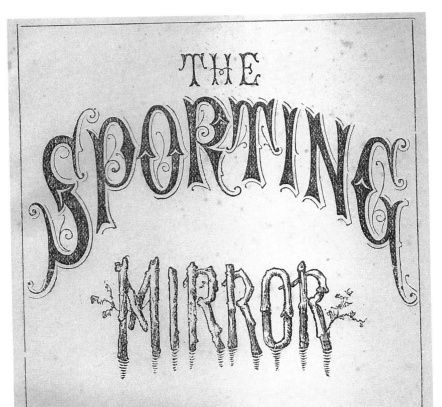

THE SPORTING MIRROR

CELEBRITIES, VOTARIES, PORTRAITS,
BIOGRAPHIES, DOINGS.

Volume VII.

JANUARY TO JUNE,

1884.

HARRY ETHERINGTON, 152, Fleet Street, London, E.C.

Albert Saxe-Coburg

Lawrence Dundas

James Hedley

William Beckwith

INDEX.

ARTICLES—   PAGE
Accuracy of Izaak Walton. By Helwr   220
Ancient and Modern Coursing. By T. Dykes   175
Athletic Training in Schools. By H. L. B.   269
Belles of the Hunt. By Plantagenet   60
Betting and Cricket. By the Man on the March   175
Billiard Tournament in America. By Anglo-Americano   ...   41
Bygone American Athletes. By Argus-Eye   276
Chasing the Leather. By H. V. L. S.   31
Coming Amateur Championship Athletic Meeting.
    By O. P. Cue   223
Coming Cricket Season. By Argus-Eye   186
Eccentric Character, An. By A. L. M.   182
Exmoor, A Day's Fishing on. By Helwr   21
Ferrets and Ferreting. By Wilf. Pocklington   199
Fourth Australian Team. By H.V.L.S.   70
German Carp Culture. By Pisciculturist   272
Jonas on Welshing. By the Man on the March   81
Leading the Hunt. By H. H. Pearse   17
Magic Circle, The. By H. Richard Butler   120
Melbourne Racecourse. By Martin Cobbett...   133
Midnight Struggle, A. By Waverley...   37
Misadventure in Melbourne, A. By Martin Cobbett   ...   73
Our Bookcase. By Old Dryasdust   48
Poachers. By T. Dykes   127
Racing on the Road. By H. B. B.   140
Shattered Idyll, A. By The Man on the March   27
Some Evils of Betting. By Martin Cobbett...   283
Some Eccentric Matches. By Argus-Eye   130
Some Hunting Thoughts. By F. M.   233
Sport and The Drama. By George L. Gordon   279
Sportsman's Exhibition. By Diomed...   147
Stanley's Pedestrian Feat. By M. R. C.   94
Story of a Yorkshire Groom   252
Sunday Cricket in the South. By Martin Cobbett   225
Tufts of Turf. By Helvellyn 116, 206, 219
Turf Siftings. By Greensward   43
Under the Burgee. By Rockwood   230
University Cricket Prospects. By Rosallian...   190
Yachting Season, The Coming. By Hold to Windward   ...   87
Notes, Dramatic and Musical. By Annotator 24, 78
Dramatic Reflections. By Conn 202, 297

PARAGRAPHS—
An Odd Name for Horses   16
Anglers' Commandments   160
Big Halibut   282
Cure for Glanders   236
Charles Cotton and Fly Fishing   185
Count Lagrange's Race-cups   189
Development of the Trotter   119
Hint to Flycasters, A   129
Hints to Dealers   62
Horse that Counts   160

PARAGRAPHS (*Continued*)—

Misuse of Technical Terms at Games	126
Novel Fox Hunting	288
Our Food Fishes	246
Paying Big Money for Cheap Trotting Stock...	114
Shyness and Timidity......	240
Speed of a Flying Duck	237
Sports Defence Association	35, 85
Successful Fisherman's Secret	139
Tench in Victoria	271
Train Delayed by Antelopes	236
University Boat Race	16
Wanton Butchery of Deer in Canada	251

PORTRAITS AND BIOGRAPHIES—

H.R.H. The Prince of Wales	1
Adams	261
Anderson, Thomas	212
Aveland, Lord	209
Beasley, Thomas	259
Beckwith, William	13
Bubear, George	57
Capp, Joseph	107
Cattlin, Charles	263
Currey, W. D. B.	174
Exeter, The Marquis of	161
Finney, James	112
Grimston, The Hon. Robert	165
Hartopp, The Late Captain	257
Hedley, Judge	9
Linde, Henry Eyre	54
McLaren, James	215
Münster, Count	105
Pitman, Frederick T.	173
Queensberry, Marquis of	49
Spencer, Earl	51
Waters, Frederick Garratt	170
Watts, John	109
Wisden, The Late John...	218
Zetland, The Earl of	5

POEMS, &c.—

Other Side of the Question, The. By H. C. Newton ...	219
May's Chief Merit. By H. C. Newton	192
Our Masher at a Boxing Competition. By J. Maycock ...	19
Talking Bird, A. By Mowbray G. Malonek	132
The Regatta Revel	268
Suspension of Pigeon Shooting, The. By J. Maycock ...	73
Undecided. By H. C. Newton	115

Issue 37 : February 1884

Portrait of Albert Saxe-Coburg (Prince of Wales)	(facing p1)
Biography - Albert Saxe-Coburg [The Turf] by HBB	(p1-4)
Portrait of Lawrence Dundas (Earl of Zetland)	(facing p5)
Biography - Lawrence Dundas [The Turf] by HBB	(p5-8)
A Few Yachting Mems	(p8)
A Notable Wrestler - Matsada Sorakichi	(p8)
Portrait of James Hedley	(facing p9)
Biography - James Hedley [Coursing] by HBB	(p9-12)
The Weather and Sport	(p12)
Dying of Thirst	(p12)
Portrait of William Beckwith	(facing p13)
Biography - William Beckwith [Swimming] by HBB	(p13-16)
Football Casualties - George Herman	(p16)
The University Boat Race	(p16)
Odd Names for Horses	(p16)
Leading the Hunt [Fiction] by Henry Pearse	(p17-18)
Our Masher at a Boxing Competition [verses] by James Maycock	(p19-20)
A Day's Fishing on Exmoor by John Roberts	(p21-23)
American Cricketers for England [The Philadelphians]	(p23)
Notes Dramatic and Musical	(p24-26)
Edward Hanlan [Sculler]	(p26)
A Shattered Idyll by Martin Cobbett	(p27-30)
Death of the Marquess de St.Sauveur	(p30)
Chasing the Leather [Association/Rugby] by Henry Stanton	(p31-34)
Cumberland & Westmoreland Wrestling Society	(p34)
Boxing in Naples	(p34)
The Sports Defence Association (part one)	(p35-36)
Death of the Marquis of Hertford (Francis Seymour)	(p36)
A Midnight Struggle [Fiction]	(p37-40)
Matthew Webb Reinterred at Niagara Falls	(p40)
A Billiard Tournament in America	(p41-42)
Turf Siftings by William Lamonby	(p43-47)
Our Bookcase :	
The Gun: Its Development (revised edition) by William Greener	(p48)
The Lion and Lamb by James Maycock	(p48)

John Douglas

John Spencer

Henry Linde

George Bubear

[Martin Cobbett (1846-1906) was one of the finest sporting journalists of his era. He started his career on *The Sporting Life* before moving to *The Sportsman* and, in 1886, to *The Referee*. He was the author of four books]

Issue 38 : March 1884

Portrait of John Douglas (Marquis of Queensberry)	(facing p49)
Biography - John Douglas [The Turf/Boxing] by HBB	(p49-50)
Portrait of John Spencer (Earl Spencer)	(facing p51)
Biography - John Spencer [Hunting] by HBB	(p51-53)
The Enthusiasm of Lady Anglers by Seth Green	(p53)
Biography - Henry Linde [The Turf] by HBB	(p54-56)
Portrait of Henry Linde	(facing p54)
Portrait of George Bubear	(facing p57)
Biography - George Bubear [Sculling] by HBB	(p57-59)
Belles of the Hunt by Ernest Pearce	(p60-62)
Skating [Safety Advice]	(p62)
A Day's Shooting on Exmoor by John Roberts	(p63-66)
A Nice Young Man - John Moran	(p66)
Theatrical Advertising - Lord Mayor's Court	(p66)
From the Wreck [verses] by Adam Lindsay-Gordon	(p67-69)
The Fourth Australian [Cricket] Team by Henry Stanton	(p70-72)
A Train Delayed by Antelopes - Union Pacific Railway	(p72)
A Misadventure in Melbourne by Martin Cobbett	(p73-76)
The Suppression of Pigeon Shooting [verses] by James Maycock	(p77)
Notes Dramatic and Musical	(p78-80)
Jonas on Welshing [Fiction] by Martin Cobbett	(p81-84)
The Sports Defence Association (part two)	(p85-86)
The Coming Yachting Season by Dixon Kemp	(p87-88)
Turf Siftings by William Lamonby	(p89-93)
Stanley's Champion Ped [Fiction] by Martin Cobbett	(p94-96)
The Sportsman's Exhibition by HBB	(p97-104)

Issue 39 : April 1884

Portrait of Georg Munster (Count Munster)	(facing p105)
Biography - Georg Munster [Coaching] by HBB	(p105-106)
Portrait of Joseph Capp	(facing p107)
Biography - Joseph Capp [Sporting Journalist] by HBB	(p107-108)
Portrait of John Watts	(facing p109)
Biography - John Watts [Jockey] by HBB	(p109-111)

Georg Munster

Joseph Capp

John Watts

James Finney

Biography - James Finney [Swimming] by HBB	(p112-114)
Portrait of James Finney	(facing p112)
Paying Big Money for Cheap Trotting Stock	(p114)
Undecided [verses] by Henry Newton	(p115)
Tufts of Turf by William Lamonby	(p116-119)
The Development of the Trotter	(p119)
The Magic Circle by Richard Butler	(p120-126)
Misuse of Technical Terms at Games by Henry Jones	(p126)
Poachers by Thomas Dykes	(p127-129)
A Hint to Fly Casters by Charles Murphy	(p129)
Some Eccentric Matches by Martin Cobbett	(p130-132)
A Rattling Burst [verses] by Mowbray Malonek	(p132)
Melbourne Racecourse at Flemington by Martin Cobbett	(p133-139)
A Successful Fisherman's Secret	(p139)
On the Road Racing by HBB	(p140-142)
An Ingenious Snake Story	(p142)
Dramatic Reflections	(p143-146)
The Sportsman's Exhibition by HBB	(p147-160)
The Angler's Commandments	(p160)
The Horse that Counts	(p160)

[Thomas Dykes was a writer for both *The Illustrated Sporting and Dramatic News* and *Country Gentleman* specialising in the turf, curling and hunting. His best known book published in 1881 was *Stories of Scottish Sport*]

Issue 40 : May 1884

Portrait of William Cecil (Marquis of Exeter)	(facing p161)
Biography - William Cecil [Yachting/Fishing] by HBB	(p161-164)
Portrait of Robert Grimston	(facing p164)
Biography - Robert Grimston [Cricket] by HBB	(p165-169)
Biography - Thomas Waters [Hunting] by HBB	(p170-172)
Portrait of Thomas Waters	(facing p170)
Portrait of William Curry	(facing p173)
Portrait of Frederick Pitman	(facing p173)
Biography - Frederick Pitman [Rowing] by HBB	(p173)
Biography - William Curry [Rowing] by HBB	(p174)
Betting and Cricket by Martin Cobbett	(p175-178)
Ancient and Modern Coursing by Thomas Dykes	(p179-181)
The Advantage of Knowing 'Natur' When You Shoot	(p181)
An Eccentric Character - Marquis of Waterford	(p182-185)

William Cecil

Robert Grimston

Thomas Waters

Gilbert Heathcote

Charles Cotton and Fly Fishing	(p185)
The Coming Cricket Season [1884] by Martin Cobbett	(p186-189)
Count Lagrange's Race Cups	(p189)
University Cricket Prospects 1884 by Martin Cobbett	(p190-191)
May's Chief Merit [verses] by Henry Newton	(p192)
Turf Siftings by William Lamonby	(p193-198)
The Value of a Carp Pond	(p198)
Ferrets and Ferreting (part one) by Wilfrid Pocklington	(p199-201)
Henry Irving as an Angler	(p201)
Book Review: *The Common Sense of Dog Doctoring* by John Walsh	(p201)
Dramatic Reflections	(p202-205)
Tufts of Turf by William Lamonby	(p206-208)

Issue 41 : June 1884

Portrait of Gilbert Heathcote (Lord Aveland)	(facing p209)
Biography - Gilbert Heathcote [Coaching] by HBB	(p209-211)
Biography - Thomas Anderson [Boxing] by HBB	(p212-214)
Portrait of Thomas Anderson	(facing p212)
Portrait of James Maclaren	(facing p215)
Biography - James Maclaren [Cricket/Rugby] by HBB	(p215-217)
Biography - John Wisden [Cricket] by HBB	(p218)
Portrait of John Wisden	(facing p218)
The Other Side of the Question [verses] by Henry Newton	(p219)
The Accuracy of Izaak Walton by James Roberts	(p220-222)
Sketch: Frith's Derby Day by Alfred Bryan	(p222)
Horse Insurance	(p222)
The Coming Amateur Champion Athletic Meeting by Robert Watson	(p223-224)
Sunday Cricket in the South [Fiction] by Martin Cobbett	(p225-229)
Canadian Grouse for Scotland	(p229)
An Expert Lady Rifle Shot - Jennie Moore	(p229)
Under the Burgee by Thomas Dykes	(p230-232)
Some Hunting Thoughts by Francis Merewether	(p233-236)
A Cure for Glanders	(p236)
About Horse-Copers by Martin Cobbett	(p237-240)
The Speed of a Flying Duck: Fifty Years with Gun and Rod	(p240)
Shyness and Timidity - Horse Language	(p240)
Ferrets and Ferreting (part two) by Wilfrid Pocklington	(p241-242)
The Philadelphian Cricketers by George Potter	(p243-246)
Our Food Fishes - The Herring by Cosser Ewart	(p246)
Tufts of Turf by William Lamonby	(p247-251)

Thomas Anderson

James Maclaren

John Wisden

Edward Hartopp

Wanton Butchery of Deer in Canada   (p251)
The Story of a Yorkshire Groom - Thomas Ward   (p252)
Dramatic Reflections   (p253-256)

Issue 42 : July 1884

Portrait of Edward Hartopp   (facing p257)
Biography - Edward Hartopp [Hunting] by HBB   (p257-258)
Portrait of Thomas Beasley   (facing p259)
Biography - Thomas Beasley [Jockey] by HBB   (p259-260)
Portrait of Joseph Adams   (facing p261)
Biography - Joseph Adams [Cycling] by HBB   (p261-262)
Portrait of Charles Cattlin   (facing p263)
Biography - Charles Cattlin [Athletics] by HBB   (p263-267)
The Regatta Revel [verses] by Henry Newton   (p268)
Athletic Training in Schools by Herbert Burrows   (p269-271)
Tench in Victoria   (p271)
German Carp Culture by Alfred Allison   (p272-275)
Bygone American Athletes by Martin Cobbett   (p276-278)
Sport and Drama by George Gordon   (p279-282)
Big Halibut   (p282)
Some Evils of Betting [Fiction] by Martin Cobbett   (p283-288)
Novel Fox Hunting   (p288)
Tufts of Turf by William Lamonby   (p289-295)
Dramatic Reflections   (p296-300)

William Currey & Frederick Pitman

Thomas Beasley

Joseph Adams

Charles Cattlin

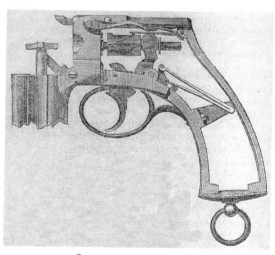

Lancaster's breech

THE SPORTING MIRROR

CELEBRITIES, VOTARIES, PORTRAITS,
BIOGRAPHIES, DOINGS.

Volume VIII.

JULY TO DECEMBER.

1884.

HARRY ETHERINGTON, 152, Fleet Street, London, E.C.

William Beauclerk

Thomas Pickernell

Herbert Speechly

William Cooper

INDEX.

ARTICLES—   PAGE

A Chat about Billiards. By Argus-Eye 124
A Chat about Scent. By Ranger 225
About French Racing. By Climax 185
A Hunting we will Go. By Hal. 261
A Forty to One Chance. By W.M.C. 181
A Piscatory Yarn. By Harry Flight 268
Betting and Backers. By Argus-Eye 33
Bear Hunting in Canada. By Ranger 64
Boxing Day with the Buckhounds 220
Decoying Snipe in America 117
Deer Hunting on the Pacific Coast. By Ranger 120
Dramatic Reflections. By Conn 44, 93, 141, 181, 237
Eighty Years Ago. By Diomed 276
Enclosed Coursing Meetings. By Humanitas 25
Health, Sport, and Exercise. By Helvellyn 3
Jack Lightman. By Martin Cobbett 15, 78, 113, 166, 209
Jockeys and Racing Weights 68
Long Scores at Cricket. By C.W.N. 86
Old Time Gambling. By Argus-Eye 233
Poachers and Poaching. By Ramrod 29
Poor Surrey Cricket Club. By the Man on the March ... 59
Road Recollections. By An Old Stager 21
Some Doncaster Reminiscences. By Helvellyn 72
Some Foxhunting Thoughts. By Clarion 171
Some Old Time Sport. By Helvellyn 37
Some Old Time Sport. By Hambletonian 133
Sport on the Kent Coast. By Wanderer 205
Thames Gudgeon Fishing. By H. L. B. 89
The Ages of Fishing. By J. H. Shaw 229
Tufts of Turf. By Helvellyn 160
Wanted, a Sporting Writer. By the Man on the March ... 40
Wildfowling in America. By J. R. Thornbury 273

BIOGRAPHIES—

Archer, Charles 204
Barrett, George 254
Beasley, Harry 49
Beasley, John 102
Bedford, C. J. 55
Birkett, W. 153
Boyce, William Dixon 250
Chaplin, Henry 244
Cooper, William Henry 12
Dawson, Matthew 199
English, R. H. 108

Index.

BIOGRAPHIES (*Continued*)—   PAGE

	PAGE
Hammond, John	145
Hill, Thomas	53
Holmes, Thomas Knox	193
Itter, Charles James	157
Keen, John	56
Legard, Sir Charles	97
Mayson, D. T.	105
Pickernell, Thomas (Mr. Thomas)	3
Rossmore, Lord	241
St. Albans, The Duke of	1
Stokes, Leonard	198
Speechly, Herbert A.	9
Webb, Frederick Edward	149

PARAGRAPHS—

	PAGE
An Elephant's Revenge	132
Crockford's Farewell	24
Fish Culture in Olden Times	92
Food Value for Fish	123
Fordham's Kidding	24
Grizzly Bear Shooting	132
Long Swims by Men and Animals	28
Not a Hound, but a Setter	123
Russian Wolfhunters	119
Slaughter of Game	136
The Deerhound and his Qualities	28

POEMS—

	PAGE
A Trill of the Twelfth. By H. Chance Newton	36
A Trolling Trill. By H. Chance Newton	140
A Winter Warble. By H. Chance Newton	219
Hold Hard. By Clarion	232
Hunting. By H. Chance Newton	176
Landing a Salmon. By Piscator	71
Leap of the Salmon	224
Pastime—Perplexity. By H. Chance Newton	58
The Three Fishers	184
The Life of a Sportsman	129
The Receipt. A Fable. By George H. Vize	163
The Staghounds	118
The Tantivy Trot. By R. E. Egerton Warburton	85
Two Sides to a Question	14

Volume Eight

August 1884 - January 1885

Issue 43 : August 1884

Portrait of William Beauclerk (Duke of St.Albans)	(facing p1)
Biography - William Beauclerk [The Turf] by HBB	(p1-2)
The Deep Sea Fishes of the Caribbean	(p2)
Portrait of Thomas Pickernell	(facing p3)
Biography - Thomas Pickernell [The Turf] by HBB	(p3-8)
Portrait of Herbert Speechly	(facing p9)
Biography - Herbert Speechly [Cycling] by HBB	(p9-11)
Biography - William Cooper [Cricket] by HBB	(p12-13)
Portrait of William Cooper	(facing p12)
Two Sides to a Question: Prejudice Speaks [verses]	(p14)
Two Sides to a Question: The Sportsman Speaks [verses]	(p14)
Jack Lightman [Fiction] (part one) by Martin Cobbett	(p15-20)
The Record of Game Killed in Austria	(p20)
Road Recollections by Stanley Harris	(p21-24)
Crockford's Farewell	(p24)
Fordham's Kidding by Robert Lyle	(p24)
Enclosed Coursing Meetings by Thomas Dykes	(p25-28)
The Deerhound and his Qualities	(p28)
Long Swims by Men and Animals	(p28)
Poachers and Poaching by John Keene	(p29-32)
The Australian Averages	(p32)
Betting and Backers by Martin Cobbett	(p33-35)
A Dream About the Melbourne Cup	(p35)
A Trill of the Twelfth [verses] by Henry Newton	(p36)
Some Old Time Sport by William Lamonby	(p37-39)
Magazine: *Wheeling* by Harry Etherington & William McWilliam	(p39)
Wanted: A Sporting Writer by Martin Cobbett	(p40-43)
Dramatic Reflections	(p44-48)

Issue 44 : September 1884

Portrait of Harry Beasley	(facing p49)
Biography - Harry Beasley [Jockey] by HBB	(p49-52)
Portrait of Thomas Hill	(facing p53)
Biography - Thomas Hill [Boxing] by HBB	(p53-55)

Harry Beasley

Thomas Hill

Charles Bedford

John Keen

Portrait of Charles Bedford (facing p55)
Charles Bedford (p55)
Biography - John Keen [Cycling] by HBB (p56-58)
Portrait of John Keen (facing p56)
Pastime Perplexity [verses] by Henry Newton (p58)
Poor Surrey Cricket Club by Martin Cobbett (p59-63)
The Best - Double Shot (p63)
Bear Hunting in Canada by Percy St.John (p64-67)
Louis XIV and Billiards (p67)
Jockeys and Racing Weights by Martin Cobbett (p68-71)
Landing a Salmon [verses] (p71)
A Cricket Umpire's Dream (p71)
Some Doncaster Reminiscences by William Lamonby (p72-77)
A Cure for Gun Shyness (p77)
Jack Lightman [Fiction] (part two) by Martin Cobbett (p78-84)
The Tantivy Trot [verses] by Roland Egerton-Warburton (p85)
Long Scores at Cricket (p86-88)
Large Dogs as Valuable Pets (p88)
Thames Gudgeon Fishing (p89-92)
Horace Davenport Swims the Solent (p92)
A Rare Ornithological Collection (p92)
Fish Culture in Olden Times (p92)
Dramatic Reflections (p93-96)

Issue 45 : October 1884

Portrait of Charles Legard (facing p97)
Biography - Charles Legard [The Turf] by HBB (p97-100)
Portrait of John Beasley (facing p101)
Biography - John Beasley [Jockey] by HBB (p101-104)
Portrait of Douglas Mayson (facing p105)
Biography - Douglas Mayson [Athletics] by HBB (p105-107)
Duck Shooting under Difficulties (p107)
Biography - Robert English [Cycling] by HBB (p108-109)
Portrait of Robert English (facing p108)
Biography - Charles Bedford [Athletics] by HBB (p110-112)
Jack Lightman [Fiction] (part three) by Martin Cobbett (p113-118)
The Staghounds [verses] (p118-119)
Russian Wolf Hunters - Moscow Hunting Club (p119)
Deer Hunting on the Pacific Coast by Percy St.John (p120-123)
Not a Hound but a Setter (p123)

Charles Legard

John Beasley

Douglas Mayson

Robert English

Food Value of Fish by Juliet Corson (p123)
A Chat About Billiards by Martin Cobbett (p124-129)
The Life of a Sportsman [verses] (p129)
Turf Red-Tapeism (p130-132)
An Elephant's Revenge (p132)
Is the Coach Dog a Pointer by Georges Buffon (p132)
Grizzly Bear Shooting (p132)
Some Old Time Sport by Thomas Smith (p133-136)
Slaughter of Game (p136)
The Trustworthiness of Charles Cotton by James Roberts (p137-139)
A Trolling Trill [verses] by Henry Newton (p140)
Dramatic Reflections (p141-144)

Issue 46 : November 1884

Portrait of John Hammond (facing p145)
Biography - John Hammond [The Turf] by HBB (p145-148)
Portrait of Frederick Webb (facing p149)
Biography - Frederick Webb [Jockey] by HBB (p149-152)
International Health Exhibition 1884 (p152)
Portrait of William Birkett (facing p153)
Biography - William Birkett [Athletics] by HBB (p153-156)
Portrait of Charles Itter (facing p157)
Biography - Charles Itter [Swimming] by HBB (p157-159)
Tufts of Turf by William Lamonby (p160-162)
The Recipe: A Fable [verses] by George Vize (p163-165)
Jack Lightman [Fiction] (part four) by Martin Cobbett (p166-170)
Some Fox Hunting Thoughts (p171-175)
Captain Floyd's Hansom Cab (p175)
Hunting [verses] by Henry Newton (p176)
Decoying Snipe in America by Percy St.John (p177-180)
A Tall Story from Forest and Stream (p180)
A Forty to One Chance [Fiction] (p181-184)
The Three Fishers [verses] (p184)
About French Racing by John Hill (p185-187)
A Horse Killing its Stable Companion (p187)
An Extraordinary Runner - Ernst Mensen (p187)
Dramatic Reflections (p188-192)

John Hammond

Frederick Webb

William Birkett

Charles Itter

Issue 47 : December 1884

Portrait of Thomas Holmes   (facing p193)
Biography - Thomas Holmes [Cycling] by HBB   (p193-197)
Prince Bismarck's Fish Preserves   (p197)
A Dog's Conscience   (p197)
Biography - Leonard Stokes [Rugby] by HBB   (p198)
Portrait of Leonard Stokes   (facing p198)
Portrait of Matthew Dawson   (facing p199)
Biography - Matthew Dawson [The Turf] by HBB   (p199-203)
Biography - Charles Archer [Jockey] by HBB   (p204)
Portrait of Charles Archer   (facing p204)
Sport on the Kent Coast by Henry Stanton   (p205-208)
Deer Hunting in Sullivan County, New York State   (p208)
Elk Hunting in Ceylon   (p208)
Jack Lightman [Fiction] (part five) by Martin Cobbett   (p209-218)
What is it? - *The Reno Gazette*   (p218)
A Winter Warble [verses] by Henry Newton   (p219)
Boxing Day with the Buckhounds by Francis Merewether   (p220-224)
Leap of the Salmon [verses] by Michael Drayton   (p224)
Old Clubs [Brookes' and Whites]   (p224)
A Chat About Scent by Percy St.John   (p225-228)
Throwing a Curb [Fiction]   (p228)
The Ages of Fishing by John Shaw   (p229-231)
Herring Fishing in the North Sea   (p231)
Hold Hard [verses]   (p232)
Old Time Gambling by Martin Cobbett   (p233-236)
Cricket Chat - Thomas Emmett   (p236)
Fishing in New South Wales   (p236)
Dramatic Reflections   (p237-240)

Issue 48 : January 1885

Portrait of Derrick Westenra (Lord Rossmore)   (facing p241)
Biography - Derrick Westenra [The Turf] by HBB   (p241-243)
Biography - Henry Chaplin [The Turf/Hunting] by HBB   (p244-249)
Portrait of Henry Chaplin   (facing p244)
Biography - William Boyce [The Turf] by HBB   (p250-253)
Portrait of William Boyce   (facing p250)
Extermination of Buffalo in Texas   (p253)
Yale College Boat Club and the English Stroke by Robert Cook   (p253)

Thomas Holmes

Leonard Stokes

Matthew Dawson

Charles Archer

Biography - George Barrett [Jockey] by HBB   (p254-258)
Portrait of George Barrett   (facing p254)
The Game of Curling by Thomas Dykes   (p259-260)
A Good Shark Story   (p260)
A Hunting We Will Go by Hal Lowther   (p261-264)
Brilliancy of a Cat's Eyes   (p264)
Room for Improvement [verses] by Henry Newton   (p265)
Health, Sport and Exercise by William Lamonby   (p266-267)
The Pugnacity of the Quail   (p267)
A Piscatory Yarn by Harry Flight   (p268-272)
Against Time   (p272)
Fishing in the Lake Superior Region by Charles Hallock   (p272)
Wildfowling in America by John Thornbury   (p273-275)
Hooking a Sandpiper   (p275)
Eighty Years Ago by HBB   (p276-279)
A Genuine Angler   (p279)
Gaffing Double   (p279)
Small Horses   (p279)
Meltonia's Gathering [verses]   (p280)
Dramatic Reflections   (p281-284)
Birds and Cholera   (p284)
Birds Drowning Fishes   (p284)

Derrick Westenra

Henry Chaplin

William Boyce

George Barrett

Archibald Montgomerie

John Clark

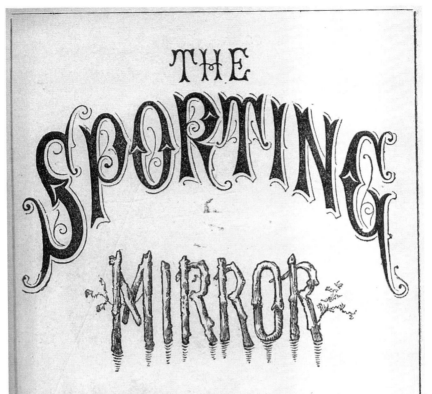

THE SPORTING MIRROR

CELEBRITIES, VOTARIES, PORTRAITS, BIOGRAPHIES, DOINGS.

Volume IX.

JANUARY TO JUNE.

1885.

HARRY ETHERINGTON, 152, Fleet Street, London, E.C.

John Dixon

Harry Kelley

Charles Manners

John Anstruther-Thomson

INDEX.

	PAGE
ARTICLES—	
A Night amongst Anglers. By H. B. Bromhead	75
About Otter Hunting. By H. P. W....	65
A Canadian Sporting Trip. By Beaver	249
A Chat about Hunters. By S. N.	167
An Equine Crack. By Argus-Eye	219
Alpine Climbing. By Wanderer	262
A Turf Experience. By Diomed	163
Fish and Fish Culture. By R. F. Shaw	18
From Epsom to Holland. By the Man on the March ...	107
Herons and Heron Shooting. By Felix Stowe	15
Horse Racing in Ancient Times. By Helvellyn	40
My Friend Inspector Johnson. By E. S.	174
Making a Hunter. By M.R.C.V.S.	32
Old Time Racing. By Argus-Eye	81
Old Time Newmarket	257
Piscatorial Tourists. By Cambria	114
Queen's Plates. By Argus-Eye	25
Salmon Life. By D. S. Jordan	170
Snipe and Snipe Shooting. By Craven	129
Some Cricket Thoughts. By Reveller	209
Some "Pikey" Chat. By J. H. K.	34
Some Sport in South Africa. By Walter Foster ... 158,	214
Sport in Maine Woods. By Ranger	134
Sport in Nova Scotia. By Ranger	22
Sportsman's Exhibition. By Diomed 187,	233
The "Plunging" Marquis. By Argus-Eye	119
The Devil upon Four Legs	253
Training Dogs and Horses. By Felix	70
Treatment of Animals, The. By Philip Vibert	273
Tufts of Turf. By Helvellyn 89, 124, 177, 223,	268
Yarns about Cougars. By Ranger	85
BIOGRAPHIES—	
Ailsa, The Marquis of	193
Barrett, Frederick	204
Beach, George	105
Bury, Viscount	145
Cannon, Joseph	62
Clark, "Judge"	3
Coombes, Richard	101
Dixon, John Edward	6
Eglinton, Earl of	1
Godwin, David	156
Hawkins, Sir Henry	241
Hewett, Walter	58
Kelley, Harry	10
Kinsky, Count Charles	97
Kynoch, George	248
Lowndes, William Selby	152
Lyttleton, Hon. Alfred	243

BIOGRAPHIES—(*continued.*)

PAGE.

Manners, Lord 49
McGeorge, Tom 100
Melgund, Viscount 149
O'Malley, Charles 196
Richards, D. 247
Squires, James Alfred 201
Thomson, Colonel Anstruther 52

DRAMATIC REFLECTIONS. By Conn. ... 43, 92, 140, 181, 236, 280

PARAGRAPHS—

Aristocratic Bruiser, An 144
Deadly Foes of the Salmon 218
English Birds in Australia 176
Equine Tips 227
Fishing in Private Waters 161
Growth of Black Bass, The 133
Hawk in an Entrance Hall 161
Irish Elk, The 21
Jump, A Big 218
Otter Hunt 176
Peculiar Fish 24
Remarkable Hen, A 69
Shooting in Canada 32
Speed of Flying Ducks 123
Stock-raising in British Columbia 173
Three Lucky Young Hunters 118
Texas Cattle King, The late 213
Turf Morality 133
Unique, Ubigue, Utique 139
Wonderful Vitality of Carp 69

POEMS—

Advice for April. By H. Chance Newton 113
Call to Cricketers, A By H. Chance Newton 208
Crack Shot, The 88
Deer's Dream, The By S. B. 137
Demoniac Drawback, A. By H. Chance Newton 279
February, Favourite, The. By H. Chance Newton ... 33
Hunter's Song, The 162
Hunting Song, A 28
Old Canoe, The 267
Racing's Reveillet. By H. Chance Newton 91
Rough on Sportsmen. By H. Chance Newton 180
Skater's Song. By St. Nicholas 32
Sportsman's Morn and Eve. By Kit Kibird 235

Volume Nine

February - July 1885

Issue 49 : February 1885

Portrait of Archibald Montgomerie (Earl of Eglinton)	(facing p1)
Biography - Archibald Montgomerie [Hunting] by HBB	(p1-2)
Portrait of John Clark	(facing p3)
Biography - John Clark [The Turf] by HBB	(p3-5)
Biography - John Dixon [Athletics] by HBB	(p6-9)
Portrait of John Dixon	(facing p6)
Biography - Harry Kelley [Rowing] by HBB	(p10-13)
Portrait of Harry Kelley	(facing p10)
The Galway Mare [verses]	(p14)
Herons and Heron Shooting by Felix Stowe	(p15-17)
Fish and Fish Culture by Robert Shaw	(p18-21)
The Irish Elk	(p21)
Sport in Nova Scotia by Percy St.John	(p22-24)
Peculiar Fish	(p24)
The Greatest Bear Fight Known [Fiction]	(p24)
Queen's Plates by Martin Cobbett	(p25-28)
A Hunting Song [verses]	(p28)
Making a Hunter	(p29-32)
Skater's Song [verses]	(p32)
Shooting in Canada	(p32)
The February Favourite [verses] by Henry Newton	(p33)
Some Pikey Chat by John Keene	(p34-39)
Killed by Wild Animals	(p39)
An Oyster Whips a Duck	(p39)
Horse Racing in Ancient Times by William Lamonby	(p40-42)
Wildfowl Shooting	(p42)
National Fish Culture Association	(p42)
Dramatic Reflections	(p43-48)
Piscatorial Dentistry	(p48)

Issue 50 : March 1885

Portrait of Charles Manners (Lord Manners)	(facing p49)
Biography - Charles Manners [The Turf] by HBB	(p49-51)
Biography - John Anstruther-Thomson [Hunting] by HBB	(p52-57)

Walter Hewitt

Joseph Cannon

Charles Kinsky

Thomas McGeorge

Portrait of John Anstruther-Thomson ..... (facing p52)
Biography - Walter Hewitt [Rowing/Rugby] by HBB ..... (p58-61)
Portrait of Walter Hewitt ..... (facing p58)
Biography - Joseph Cannon [The Turf] by HBB ..... (p62-64)
Portrait of Joseph Cannon ..... (facing p62)
About Otter Hunting ..... (p65-69)
A Remarkable Hen by Frank Hill ..... (p69)
Wonderful Vitality of Carp by Milton Price ..... (p69)
Training Dogs and Horses by Rawdon Lee ..... (p70-74)
O Tempora! O Mores! [verses] ..... (p74)
A Night Amongst Anglers by HBB ..... (p75-80)
The Cruelty of Fox Hunting by George Rooper ..... (p80)
A Large Haul of Sardines ..... (p80)
Old Time Racing by Martin Cobbett ..... (p81-84)
High Price for a Spaniel ..... (p84)
Yarns About Cougars by Percy St.John ..... (p85-88)
The Crack Shot [verses] ..... (p88)
Tufts of Turf by William Lamonby ..... (p89-90)
Racing's Reveille [verses] by Henry Newton ..... (p91)
Dramatic Reflections ..... (p92-96)

Issue 51 : April 1885

Portrait of Charles Kinsky (Count Kinsky) ..... (facing p97)
Biography - Charles Kinsky [Gentleman Rider] by HBB ..... (p97-99)
Biography - Thomas McGeorge [The Turf] by HBB ..... (p100)
Portrait of Thomas McGeorge ..... (facing p100)
Portrait of Richard Coombes ..... (facing p101)
Biography - Richard Coombes [Athletics] by HBB ..... (p101-104)
Portrait of George Beach ..... (facing p105)
Biography - George Beach [Sculling] by HBB ..... (p105-106)
From Epsom to Holland by Martin Cobbett ..... (p107-112)
Canine Instinct ..... (p112)
A Baby Camel ..... (p112)
Advice for April [verses] by Henry Newton ..... (p113)
Piscatorial Tourists ..... (p114-118)
Three Lucky Young Hunters ..... (p118)
The Plunging Marquis by Martin Cobbett ..... (p119-123)
The Speed of Flying Ducks by Richard Winans ..... (p123)
Tufts of Turf by William Lamonby ..... (p124-128)
Dogs Faithful Unto Death ..... (p128)

Richard Coombes

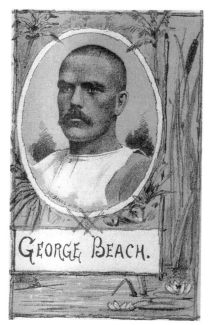

George Beach

William Keppel

Gilbert Kynynmound

Snipe and Snipe Shooting by John Manley (p129-133)
The Growth of Black Bass (p133)
Turf Morality by Charles Greville (p133)
Sport in the Maine Woods by Percy St.John (p134-136)
The Deer's Dream [verses] (p137-139)
Fishing From Thames Weir Heads (p139)
Unique, Ubique, Utique (p139)
Dramatic Reflections (p140-144)
An Aristocratic Bruiser - Tatton Sykes (p144)

Issue 52 : May 1885

Portrait of William Keppel (Viscount Bury) (facing p145)
Biography - William Keppel [Cycling] by HBB (p145-148)
Palmerston, Pugilism and Politics (p148)
Portrait of Gilbert Kynynmound (Viscount Melgund) (facing p149)
Biography - Gilbert Kynynmound [The Turf] by HBB (p149-151)
Biography - William Selby-Lowndes [Hunting] by HBB (p152-155)
Portrait of William Selby-Lowndes (facing p153)
Unwholesome Fish in London (p155)
Dairy Farming in Canada (p155)
Biography - David Godwin [Sculling] by HBB (p156-157)
Portrait of David Godwin (facing p156)
Some Sport in South Africa (part one) by Walter Foster (p158-161)
Fishing in Private Waters (p161)
A Hawk in an Entrance Hall (p161)
The Hunter's Song [verses] (p162)
A Turf Experience by HBB (p163-166)
A Chat About Hunters (p167-169)
The Japanese Consul and his Penchant for Dogs (p169)
Salmon Life by David Jordan (p170-173)
Stock Raising in British Columbia (p173)
Fred Archer in a Fight (p173)
My Friend Inspector Johnson [Fiction] (p174-176)
English Birds in Australia (p176)
Otter Hunt (p176)
Tufts of Turf by William Lamonby (p177-179)
Manchester Racecourse Committee (p179)
Baden-Baden Races 1885 (p179)
Frank Carver Shooting Bats in New Orleans (p179)
Rough on Sportsmen [verses] by Henry Newton (p180)

William Selby-Lowndes

David Godwin

Archibald Kennedy

Charles O'Malley

Dramatic Reflections (p181-186)
Vermin in Stables (p186)
Stranding of a Whale in the River Severn (p186)
The Sportsman's Exhibition by HBB (p187-192)

Issue 53 : June 1885

Portrait of Archibald Kennedy (Marquis of Ailsa) (facing p193)
Biography - Archibald Kennedy [Yachting] by HBB (p193-195)
Biography - Charles O'Malley [Rowing/Athletics] by HBB (p196-200)
Portrait of Charles O'Malley (facing p196)
Portrait of James Squires (facing p201)
Biography - James Squires [Athletics] by HBB (p201-203)
Biography - Frederick Barrett [Jockey] by HBB (p204-207)
Portrait of Frederick Barrett (facing p204)
Horses and Work: Review - *Horses of the Sahara* by Eugene Daumas (p207)
A Call to Cricketers [verses] by Henry Newton (p208)
Some Cricket Thoughts by John Heywood (p209-213)
Amusing Reproof to Sunday Anglers (p213)
The Late Texas Cattle King - Richard King (p213)
Some Sport in South Africa (part two) by Walter Foster (p214-218)
A Big Jump - Punchestown (p218)
The Deadly Foes of the Salmon by Stephen Ellis (p218)
An Equine Crack by Martin Cobbett (p219-222)
Catching His Fish and then Buying Them (p222)
Tufts of Turf by William Lamonby (p223-227)
An Australian on Shaw's Team by Tom Horan (p227)
Equine Tips (p227)
Sporting in Wisconsin by Percy St.John (p228-231)
The Sportsman's Exhibition by HBB (p232-234)
Sportsman's Morn and Eve [verses] by William Percy (p235)
Dramatic Reflections (p236-240)
Buildings That Resist Earthquakes (p240)

Issue 54 : July 1885

Portrait of Henry Hawkins (facing p241)
Biography - Henry Hawkins [The Turf] by HBB (p241-242)
A Long Walk (p242)
Portrait of Alfred Lyttelton (facing p243)
Biography - Alfred Lyttelton [Cricket] by HBB (p243-246)

James Squires

Frederick Barrett

Henry Hawkins

Alfred Lyttelton

Australia as a Boating Centre	(p246)
Portrait of David Richards	(facing p247)
Biography - David Richards [Billiards] by HBB	(p247)
Biography - George Kynoch [Shooting] by HBB	(p248)
Portrait of George Kynoch	(facing p248)
A Canadian Sporting Trip by Percy St.John	(p249-252)
The Devil Upon Four Legs [Fiction]	(p253-256)
Another Pugilistic Sensation	(p256)
The Bicycle Thief	(p256)
Old Time Newmarket by Martin Cobbett	(p257-261)
The Laws of Duelling	(p261)
Alpine Climbing by Henry Stanton	(p262-266)
A Noted Woodchuck Dog	(p266)
Running - *Book of Health* by Malcolm Morris	(p266)
The Old Canoe [verses]	(p267)
Tufts of Turf by William Lamonby	(p268-272)
The Treatment of Horses by Philip Vibert	(p273-278)
A Dog's Home in Moscow	(p278)
A Poacher's Grievance	(p278)
A Demoniac Drawback [verses] by Henry Newton	(p279)
Dramatic Reflections	(p280-284)
High Price for a Setter Puppy by Percy Ohl	(p284)
A Wagtail's Nest	(p284)

David Richards

George Kynoch

ETON VERSUS HARROW. OR

This performance always commands a good audience

The "Lion" with the Fair Sex.

"EATING" VERSUS CRICKET

Would go anywhere to see a day's Cricket.

HOW THEY SAW THE MATCH.

SIT DOWN

A sad but true Incident.

Enthusiasts.

HG Banks del

THE SPORTING MIRROR

CELEBRITIES, VOTARIES, PORTRAITS, BIOGRAPHIES, DOINGS.

Volume X.

JULY TO DECEMBER.

1885.

PUBLISHED FOR THE PROPRIETORS BY

A. PALMER & SON, 12, PATERNOSTER ROW, E.C.

Sketches at SANDOWN

Lord Marcus

Archer invigorating himself with an orange.

The saddling of the Bard attracts the noble Sportsmen

In the Paddock

A few Well Known forms.

INDEX.

ARTICLES—
PAGE

A Creel Full. By Helwr 272
A Day in the Country. By a Criminal at Large 20
A Hunt Breakfast. By Diomed 172
A Trout's Tale. By S. Farie 87
Barbel, and Barbel-fishing. By H. B. Bromhead 65
Big Sport with Duck. By Barney 268
Boar Hunting. By Colonel P. 9
Boar Hunting Experiences. By Ranger 153
Breeding in England and America. By Privateer 26
Doncaster Deductions. By Argus-Eye 69
Dramatic Reflections. By Conn 43, 91, 188, 236, 276
Early Days out West. By Pintail 37
Fen Skating. By H. B. Bromhead... 257
Grouse and Partridge Driving. By G. H. Manley, M.A. ... 119
Kempton Park. By Diomed 165
My First Pike. By J. R. Roberts 252
My Friend the Master. By J. R. Roberts 220
Newmarket Notions. By Argus-Eye 136
Newmarket Houghton. By Argus-Eye 167
November's Sport. By the Man in Green... 160
Our National Pastime. By H. B. Bromhead 177, 208
Old Time Coursing. By Wanderer... 113
Partridge Shooting near Tangier. By Fraximus 243
Sandown Park. By Diomed... 55
Shark Fishing. By Colin 261
Snipe and Woodcock. By J. J. Manley 214
Some Football Chat. By G. F. C. 225
Some Hunting Talk. By Whiz 264
Sport on Loch Leven 102
Sport in South Africa. By Walter Foster... 81
Sporting Chat and Anecdote... 248
Sporting Fixtures for 1886 282
Thames Angling. By H. B. Bromhead 107
Thames Gudgeoning. By H. B. Bromhead 5
The Red Deer of Killarney. By H. A. Herbert 58
Those Purple Moors. By Organist... 74
Thoughts of Goodwood. By Argus-Eye 33
Tufts of Turf. By Helvellyn 12, 52, 131, 184, 204
Walrus Hunting. By Frederick Schwatka 103
Winter Fishing. By J. H. K. 200
With An Old Sportsman. By Diomed 231
Yachting, and the American Cup. By Jack Yard 123

Index.

BIOGRAPHIES AND BIOGRAPHY—   PAGE

	PAGE
Beresford, Lord Charles	196
Brett, Colonel Sir Wilford	49
Bradford, Earl of	145
Carrington, Lord	193
Chetwynd, Sir George	97
Goodall, Frank	241
Wombwell, Sir George	1

PARAGRAPHS—

A Fishy Invention	117
A Fish Story	112
A New Stud Horse	271
A Record Breaker	112
A Sporting Club	271
A Tip to Horse Drivers	86
An Impromptu	64
An American Sporting Club	199
Cavendish Club Coursing Meeting	207
Chantilly Racecourse	50
Dairy Farming	182
Death of Mr. T. V. Morgan	260
Death of Mr. W. H. Vanderbilt	256
Deer Stalking	203
Enclosed Coursing in America	139
Fishing for Swordfish off Nova Scotia	219
How to Test Milk	64
Hunting the Wild Cattle of Jersey	117
Insect Enemies	4
International Swimming Competition	11
Jack Mytton's Daughter.	247
Lady Athletes	271
November Notes	183
"Old Clubfoot," the Grizzly, Killed	106
Otter Hunting	152
Prince Henry of Battenberg	139
Presentation to Mr. Fred Gallaher	240
Racing Times	281
Salmon in British Columbia	117
Sharp Practice	164
Sprinting in Australia	100
The Grand Prix de Paris	256
The Ruling Passion	64
The Thames at Richmond	64

POEMS—

A Good Reason. By H. Chance Newton	51
December Doings. By H. Chance Newton	213
Eton and Harrow. By H. Chance Newton	18
Football Ferocity. By H. Chance Newton	13_5

Volume Ten

August 1885 - January 1886

Issue 55 : August 1885

Portrait of George Wombwell	(facing p1)
Biography - George Wombwell [Hunting] by HBB	(p1-4)
Insect Enemies: Wet Worm in Kansas	(p4)
Thames Gudgeoning by HBB	(p5-8)
Boar Hunting by Coulson Pitman	(p9-11)
International Swimming Competition: Berlin Swimming Union	(p11)
Tufts of Turf by William Lamonby	(p12-17)
Eton and Harrow [verses] by Henry Newton	(p18-19)
Lithograph: *Eton versus Harrow*	(facing p18)
Beach says he is the Tomki - Rowing	(p19)
A Day in the Country [Fiction]	(p20-25)
Breeding in England and America by Charles Foster	(p26-32)
Thames Angling Preservation Society	(p32)
Thoughts of Goodwood by Martin Cobbett	(p33-36)
Early Days Out West	(p37-42)
Dramatic Reflections	(p43-48)

Issue 56 : September 1885

Portrait of Wilford Brett	(facing p49)
Biography - Wilford Brett [The Turf] by HBB	(p49-50)
Chantilly Racecourse	(p50)
A Good Reason [verses] by Henry Newton	(p51)
Tufts of Turf by William Lamonby	(p52-54)
Lithograph: *Sketches at Sandown*	(facing p55)
Sandown Park by HBB	(p55-57)
Poole Mackerel Fishery	(p57)
The Red Deer of Killarney by George Herbert	(p58-64)
An Impromptu [verses] by Zaida Erskine	(p64)
How to Test Milk	(p64)
The Ruling Passion	(p64)
Barbel and Barbel Fishing by HBB	(p65-68)
The Thames at Richmond	(p68)
Doncaster Deductions by Martin Cobbett	(p69-73)

George Wombwell

Wilford Brett

George Chetwynd

Orlando Bridgeman

Irish Fishery Conservators (p73)
Those Purple Moors [with verses] (p74-80)
Take Care of the Pence - Marquis of Hertford (p80)
Rearing Colts (p80)
Some Sport in South Africa (part three) by Walter Foster (p81-86)
A Tip to Horse Owners (p86)
A Trout's Tale (p87-90)
Dramatic Reflections (p91-96)

Issue 57 : October 1885

Portrait of George Chetwynd (facing p97)
Biography - George Chetwynd [The Turf] by HBB (p97-102)
Sport on Loch Leven (p102)
Walrus Hunting by Frederick Schwatka (p103-106)
Old Clubfoot the Grizzly Killed (p106)
Sprinting in Australia (p106)
Thames Angling by HBB (p107-112)
A Record Breaker: Dumb-Bells (p112)
A Fish Story by Dorsey French (p112)
Old Time Coursing by Henry Stanton (p113-117)
Hunting the Wild Cattle of New Jersey (p117)
Salmon in British Columbia (p117)
A Fishy Invention (p117)
Grouse and Partridge Driving by John Manley (p118-122)
Yachting and the America's Cup by Dixon Kemp (p123-130)
Performances of the Leger Winner (p130)
Lithograph: *His First Appearance in the Pig-Skin* (facing p131)
Tufts of Turf by William Lamonby (p131-134)
A Magnificent Kennel - Pierre Lorillard's (p134)
Football Ferocity [verses] by Henry Newton (p135)
Newmarket Notions by Martin Cobbett (p136-139)
Prince Henry of Battenburg (p139)
Enclosed Coursing in America [at Newark] (p139)
Dramatic Reflections (p140-144)

Issue 58 : November 1885

Portrait of Orlando Bridgeman (Earl of Bradford) (facing p145)
Biography - Orlando Bridgeman [The Turf] by HBB (p145-152)
Otter Hunting [verses] (p152)

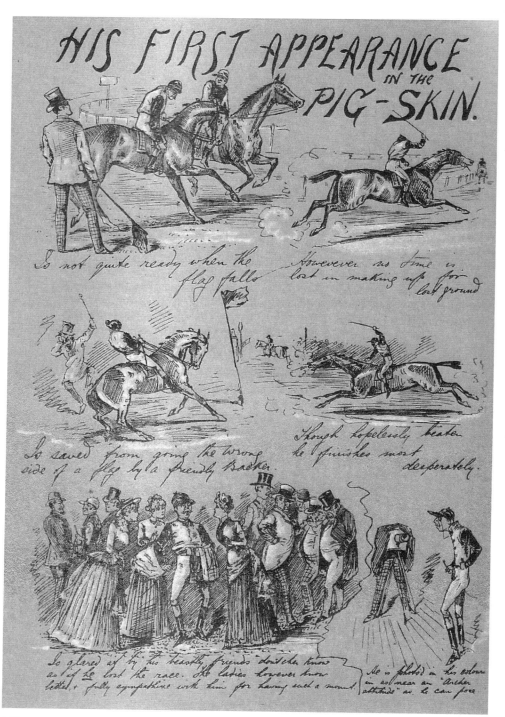

HIS FIRST APPEARANCE IN THE PIG-SKIN.

Is not quite ready when the flag falls

Howvever as time is lost in making up for lost ground

Is saved from going the wrong side of a flag by a friendly backer.

Though hopelessly beaten he finishes most desperately.

Is glared at by his beastly friends "don't cha know" as if he lost the race. The ladies however know better, & fully sympathise with him for having such a mount

He is photo'd in his colours in as near an "Archer" attitude as he can force

Bear Hunting Experiences by Percy St.John (p153-159)
An Indian Village at the Albert Palace (p159)
November's Sport by Martin Cobbett (p160-164)
Sharp Practice (p164)
Lithograph: *In the Paddock at Kempton Park* (facing p165)
Kempton Park by HBB (p165-166)
Newmarket Houghton by Martin Cobbett (p167-171)
A Hunt Breakfast by HBB (p172-176)
Our National Pastime (part one) by HBB (p177-182)
Dairy Farming - Short Horn Company (p182)
November Notes [verses] by Henry Newton (p183)
Tufts of Turf by William Lamonby (p184-187)
Dramatic Reflections (p188-192)

Issue 59 : December 1885

Portrait of Charles Carington (Lord Carrington) (facing p193)
Biography - Charles Carington [The Turf] by HBB (p193-195)
Ladies Hunting Habits [Meath Hunt] (p195)
A New Method of Propulsion of Vessels (p195)
Biography - Charles Beresford [The Navy] by HBB (p196-199)
Portrait of Charles Beresford (facing p196)
An American Sporting Club by Pierre Lorillard (p199)
Winter Fishing by John Keene (p200-203)
Deer Stalking (p203)
The Australian Cricket Eleven 1886 (p203)
The Colquhoun Sculls (p203)
Tufts of Turf by William Lamonby (p204-207)
Cavendish Club Coursing Meeting (p207)
Our National Pastime (part two) by HBB (p208-212)
Inbreeding (p212)
December Doings [verses] by Henry Newton (p213)
Snipe and Woodcock by John Manley (p214-219)
Fishing for Swordfish off Nova Scotia (p219)
International Pistol Match at Vienna (p219)
Sport in the Highlands (p219)
My Friend The Master by James Roberts (p220-224)
Ascent of the Jungfrau (p224)
Some Football Chat [Folk Football] (p225-230)
Marine Fish Culture (p230)
With An Old Sportsman by HBB (p231-235)

IN THE PADDOCK.
KEMPTON PARK

THE POPULAR SECRETARY.

CAPTAIN BAYLEY.

G. EVERETT.

GRAPH OFFICE

"All right"

Wildfowl on the Thames by John Bickerdyke (p235)
Dramatic Reflections (p236-240)
Coursing in Ancient Times by Thomas Elliot (p240)
Presentation to Frederick Gallaher - Irish Athletic Team (p240)
To The Bitter End (p240)

Issue 60 : January 1886

Portrait of Frank Goodall (facing p241)
Biography - Frank Goodall [Hunting] by HBB (p241-242)
Partridge Shooting Near Tangier (p243-247)
Jack Mytton's Daughter - South Cheshire Hounds (p247)
Sporting Chat and Anecdote by HBB (p248-251)
My First Pike by James Roberts (p252-256)
Death of William Vanderbilt (p256)
The Grand Prix de Paris (p256)
Fen Skating by HBB (p257-260)
Death of Thomas Morgan (p260)
Shark Fishing by Colin Taylor (p261-263)
Some Hunting Talk by HBB (p264-267)
Caulking Seams (p267)
Vanished Dog Stars (p267)
Big Sport With Duck (p268-271)
Lady Athletes [in Ootacamund] (p271)
A New Stud Horse (p271)
A Creel Full by James Roberts (p272-275)
Dramatic Reflections (p276-281)
Racing Times (p281)
Sporting Fixtures :
        The Turf (p282-283)
        Lawn Tennis (p284)
        Coursing (p284)

Charles Carington

Charles Beresford

Frank Goodall

Harry Etherington wearing the club cap of the Temple Bicycle Club of London